Seasons of Celebrations

AVE MARIA PRESS
NOTRE DAME, INDIANA 46556

International Standard Book Number: 0-87793-566-1

Library of Congress Catalog Number: 95-77475

Cover, text design and illustrations by Katherine Robinson Coleman

Printed and bound in the United States of America.

Dedicated to catechists everywhere
who share the good news
of Jesus Christ
with others.

Contents

Introduction ~9~

Chapter 1 ~Advent~ We Prepare for Jesus ~12~

Chapter 2 ~Christmas~ We Celebrate God's Love ~40~

Chapter 3 ~Lent~ We Change Our Lives ~70~

Contents *(continued)*

Introduction

Through feasts and seasons of the liturgical year we learn about God's presence in our lives, in our world, in our church community, and in one another. We recall all that God has done for us and we praise God's name. The activities in this book encourage children to explore who they are as Christians as they journey through the Church Year.

The focus of this book is to help the students discover how they are to live their faith in God. The emphasis of each activity is on engaging the interest of the students and actively involving them so that they will remember what they have learned after they leave the classroom.

A variety of activities are included so as to appeal to many different personalities, types, and ages of students. The activities are primarily designed to benefit elementary age children. Many of the activities can also be used successfully to enrich the learning experience of preschool and middle school students.

Seasons of the Church Year

The book follows the order of the Church Year and contains a wealth of ideas for each season. Chapters are included on Advent, Christmas, Lent, Easter, and Ordinary Time.

The activities in the first chapter encourage children to explore Advent, the four-week season of hopeful expectation. We wait for Christmas and coming of the light of Christ into our lives. We prepare for Christ by the way we treat one another.

Christmas is the season of joy and giving modeled in God's great gift of his Son, Jesus Christ. Many of the ideas in Chapter 2 are service-oriented. They help the children share the love of God with others. Activities for celebrating the feast of Epiphany are also included in this chapter.

Lent is the season of growth and renewal. Activities in Chapter 3 teach the children to learn about God's actions in our lives. Also included in this chapter are Holy Week activities which help children clearly understand the culmination of the events of Lent, the offering of Jesus' life on behalf of all.

The darkness of Lent is transformed into the great feast of the resurrection and the beautiful fifty-day Easter season. Chapter 4 activities help the children to express creatively the good news that "He is risen!" Activities are also included in this chapter for celebrating the coming of the Holy Spirit at Pentecost.

The activities in Chapter 5 express the uniqueness of Ordinary Time. They help children live their faith as children of the Father and followers of Jesus through the Holy Spirit. Ideas centered on common gospel themes for the season are included as well as activities based on the lives of saints whose feast days are celebrated during Ordinary Time.

Who Can Use the Book

Seasons of Celebrations lends itself to children's joyful participation in learning activities designed with them in mind. The activities are flexible and easy to use. They supplement a variety of religion courses and can be used in many different situations in parishes, schools, and homes.

Religious education programs will be enriched through the wide variety of ideas that appeal to many different types of children from different backgrounds. Working on these projects with fellow students helps each person to get to know one another as members of a parish community. The action of "doing" gives these children a sense that they are vital members of the family of faith.

Seasons of Celebrations works well in parochial schools because of the multiple choice of activities for each season. For example, each grade level can engage in a different activity related to one season. This avoids the problem of students losing interest when the same activity is repeated year after year.

Summer programs will also benefit from this book because the activities encourage the children's interest in learning. Not only are activities from the Ordinary Time chapter appropriate for summer program students; Advent, Christmas, Lent, and Easter crafts and projects can be planned and produced in preparation for the coming school year.

Other programs and learning situations that can benefit from using the nursery and preschool activities in *Seasons of Celebrations* include:

Nursery and preschool programs. Teachers and parents of preschool children will find that these ideas help young children learn the basic concepts of their Christian faith in a way they can understand.

After-school programs. Working on projects of this type engages the interest of children even after a long day at school and makes learning by doing a fun experience.

Family projects. Families can work together on these activities at home with a minimum of preparation in their busy lives. Enough ideas are offered to help them joyfully explore each season of the Church Year.

Sacrament preparation programs. These activities help personalize learning for the students and encourage them to live their faith.

Lectionary-based catechetical programs. Project ideas are offered for all three cycles of the Church Year.

Family formation programs. A difficult part of organizing family formation programs is planning for many different grade levels. The activities in this book appeal to a wide age range of children, but are theologically sound for adult learning also.

Children's liturgy of the word. The ideas can be implemented to help children understand the Sunday readings and how they are able to enact them in their own lives.

Home schooling. Children who are taught at home will be delighted to engage in interesting activities to supplement the regular curriculum used by their parents.

Children's liturgies. The liturgical environment and liturgy itself can be enhanced with prayers, banners, projects, and other activities described in this resource. Many of the projects are related to liturgical themes.

The activities described in the following chapters offer children opportunities to engage themselves in the joy, spirit, mood, and themes of each season. Participation in these individual activities encourages a larger scale participation in the church community itself. The Church Year is a wonderful gift that God has given us. Through celebrating as a community we learn to join together and live what we believe. We are renewed as we follow Jesus Christ through each season of the year.

Chapter 1

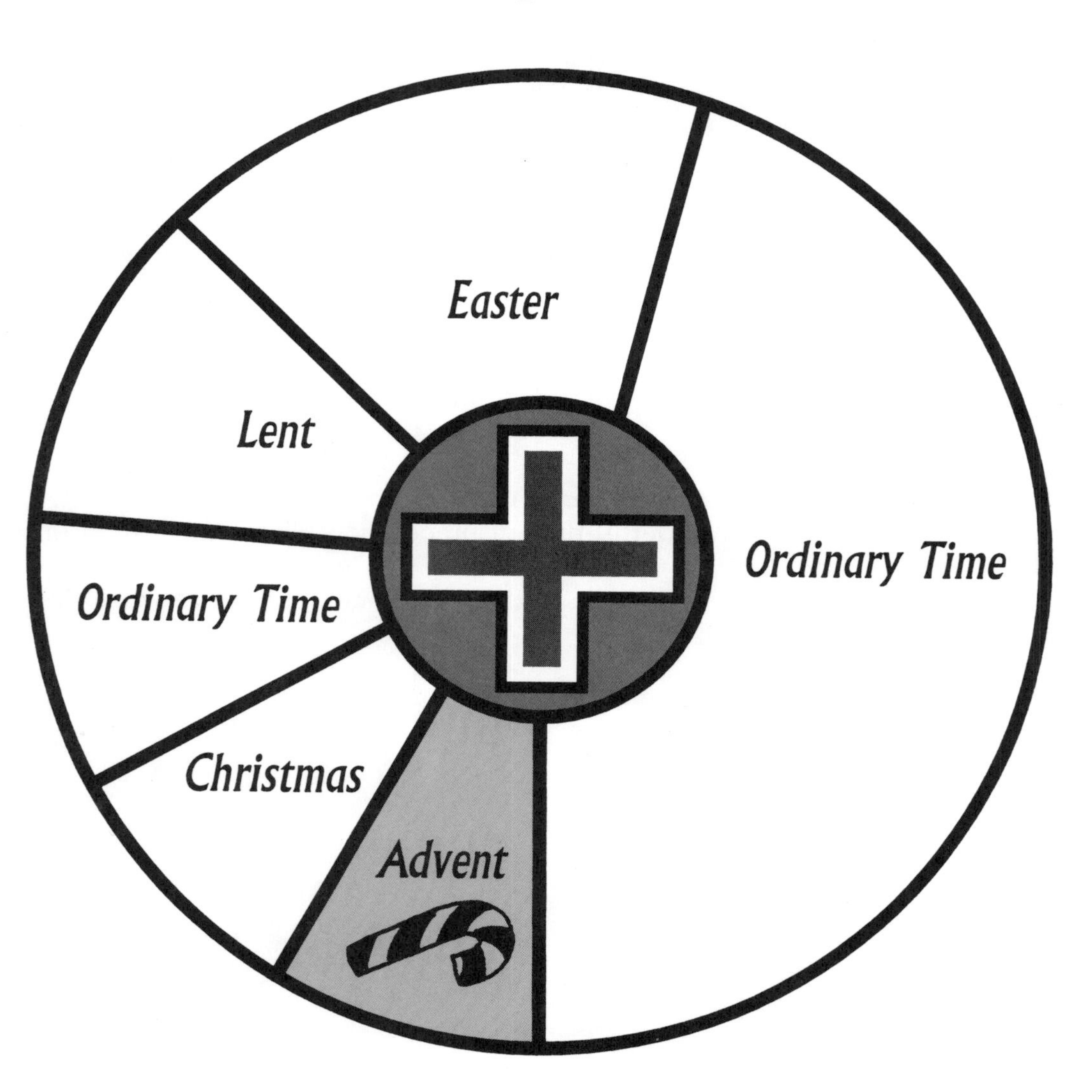

~Advent~

We Prepare for Jesus

He will be great
and will be called
Son of the Most High.

Advent is the first season of the Church Year. It is a four week season of hope and expectation. It is a wonderful time of preparation for the great feast of Christmas.

Advent is a time of reflecting on all that the coming of Jesus means to us and to the world. We are to live Advent. We are to reach out to others during this season and bring them hope. We are to share God's love.

The scripture readings for the first half of Advent speak to us of hope for the future. We focus on the coming of Jesus at the end of time. We live in constant hope and expectation of living with Jesus in glory.

The readings for the second half of Advent focus on the coming of Jesus at Bethlehem. God's promise to his people was fulfilled in a way more glorious that anyone could have expected: "For God so loved the world that he gave his only Son" (John 3:16). We celebrate all that Jesus' coming means to us.

Jesus is the light of the world. The candles that we light during Advent remind us of his coming as the light of our lives. Uncovering these themes of Advent helps children learn that they are to follow him always in all things. Through prayer, service, and participation, children learn the fruits of living in hopeful expectation of the Messiah. Come, Lord Jesus.

Advent Wreath

The tradition of the Advent wreath helps us pray together during this holy season. Each of the four candles of the Advent wreath represents one of the weeks of Advent.

The candles of the wreath light the way to Christmas. As the light from more candles grows brighter, Christmas draws nearer. The Advent wreath reminds us that God is always faithful. God's promise is always fulfilled. God loves us with an unending love.

The following prayers can be used with children each week of Advent. Choose one student to read the prayer. Ask the others to say the response.

First Week of Advent (light one purple candle)

Reader: God, we wait for the coming of your Son, Jesus, into our hearts and our lives this Advent. Help us to always follow him as the light of the world.

Response: **We give you thanks and praise.**

Second Week of Advent (light two purple candles)

Reader: God, we look forward to Christmas and the joy it brings. Help us to share our happiness with others during this Advent season.

Response: **We give you thanks and praise.**

Third Week of Advent (light two purple candles and one pink)

Reader: God, as Christmas draws nearer we decorate our homes in preparation for the birthday of Jesus. Help us remember always that Jesus is the reason for our celebration.

Response: **We give you thanks and praise.**

Fourth Week of Advent (light all four candles)

Reader: God, during this Advent season we prepare our hearts for the coming of Jesus. Help us to be the kind of people you created us to be now and throughout the year.

Response: **We give you thanks and praise.**

Waiting Song

Young children enjoy singing songs as a way of learning about the seasons of the Church Year. The following song about Advent is sung to the tune of "Mary Had a Little Lamb".

Advent is a time to share,
time to share, time to share.
Advent is a time to share
while we wait for Jesus.

Advent is a time to pray,
time to pray, time to pray.
Advent is a time to pray
while we wait for Jesus.

Advent is a time to love,
time to love, time to love.
Advent is a time to love
while we wait for Jesus.

Singing is a joyful experience for children and a great learning activity. This song helps children understand that Advent is a time of waiting and a time of getting ready for the coming of Jesus.

Burlap Banner

Individual burlap banners made by the children as an Advent project are great for display at home or to use as a Christmas gift.

Purchase burlap at a fabric store by the yard. Cut one 9″ x 13″ piece for each child. Fold the top inch of a width edge and sew to make a rod pocket. Fringe the other three sides of the burlap before class begins.

Have the children glue two pieces of green ric-rac onto the banner: one piece horizontally across the middle of the banner and the other piece vertically. This divides the banner into four sections.

Each week have the children cut out one felt symbol to connect to one section of their banner. Symbols may include things like a green tree, red bell, yellow star, and blue stocking. If necessary, provide patterns for them to use. Have the students use craft glue to connect their symbols to the banner. Craft glue does not soak through the felt and provides for a better finished project.

When completed, put a 10″ wooden dowel through the rod pocket. A 20″ length of green yarn can be tied by the students to the ends of the dowel as a hanger.

This project helps children count the weeks of Advent as they wait for Christmas day.

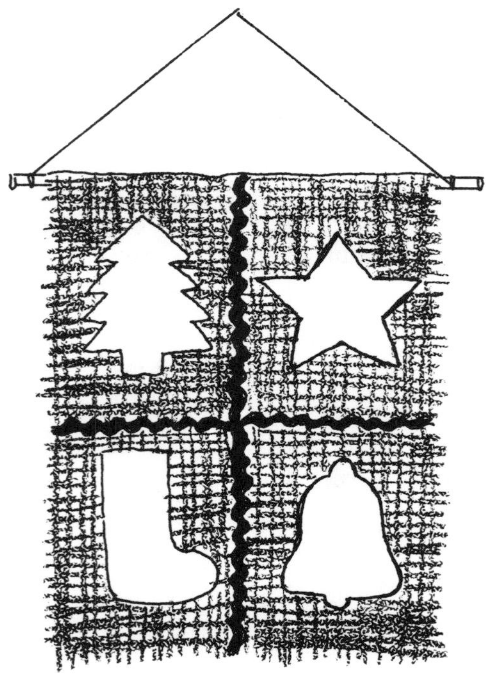

Candy Canes

December 6 is the feast of St. Nicholas, patron saint of children. Give candy canes to the children in celebration of his feast day. To make these candy canes special, tie a card printed with *The Legend of the Candy Cane* to each one.

Before class print or type the following words of the candy cane legend. Include a drawing or sticker of a candy cane in the margin for decoration.

~The Legend of the Candy Cane~

We give you this candy cane
to celebrate St. Nicholas.
His feast day is December 6.
St. Nicholas is the patron
saint of children. He was also a
bishop in Greece. This candy
cane is shaped like his bishop's staff.

Happy St. Nicholas Day!

Duplicate the legend for each child on heavy paper or card stock. Cut the stories apart. Use a hole punch to make a hole in the upper left corner of each copy. Cut a length of red yarn and thread the yarn through the hole. Tie the legend around the candy cane with a bow.

Put all the candy canes in a basket and let each child take one home. This is a special treat and a nice reminder of the feast of St. Nicholas. St. Nicholas is a great example to the children of the spirit of sharing that should be a part of our lives during Advent and the rest of the year.

Stocking Service Project

Community and service organizations often sponsor a party for young children in need during the Advent season. These parties feature food, gifts, and a visit by Santa Claus. Make a wonderful contribution to such an occasion by providing the guests with gift stockings.

Felt stockings can be sewn for each child or inexpensive net stockings can be purchased for this project. All stockings should be the same.

Ask students to bring appropriate items to fill the stockings. Send a note to parents enlisting support for this project. Remind children and parents that items must be small enough to fit in a stocking and appropriate for both boys and girls. Provide a list of suitable items for the stockings such as:

- small toys
- stuffed animals
- markers
- crayons
- coloring books
- pencils
- games
- snow scenes
- candy canes
- toy watches
- gift certificates
- wind-up toys

Provide collection boxes for the items. Then have a team of children and adults available to fill the stockings. Arrange a time for delivery.

Several classes or groups can work together on this project. One group can sew the stockings, one can provide the items, and another fill the stockings and deliver them.

This is a great service project because it benefits children with special needs. Spreading joy to children is an important part of the Advent season.

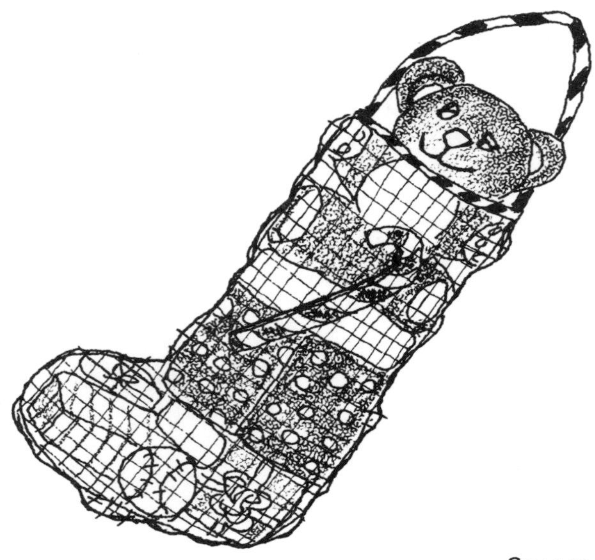

Blessings Prayer

The following prayer can be used with children during Advent. It helps children capture the hopeful spirit of the Advent season. Print the prayer on a large classroom poster. Encourage recitation often during Advent.

Loving God,
We give you thanks for the blessings
  of this holy Advent season.
You are the source of life, of hope,
  and of all good things.

We look forward to the coming
  of the light of Christ at Christmas.
Help us to turn toward that light
  in our lives.

We rejoice at the gift of your Son
  who taught us to love in your name.
May we be people of peace and justice
  all the days of our lives.

Your kingdom come and your will be done
  now and forever.

Amen.

Advent Activities

The Advent season is a time of reaching out to others with love and care.

Children must understand that during this season they too are called to help others. Discuss with the students ways they can reach out to others. Encourage students to contribute their own ideas. Advent opportunities for service include:

- praying for people in need
- giving blankets to the homeless
- introducing a new child to others
- sending Christmas greeting cards
- trimming a tree at a nursing home
- treating others with respect
- baking cookies and giving them away
- helping a younger child with schoolwork
- contributing to a children's hospital
- celebrating the sacrament of reconciliation
- sharing belongings with a friend.

These and other actions help children live the spirit of love, the spirit of the Advent season. Use these actions as starting points for reflection on the kind of people God calls us to be.

Isaiah Reading

It is important for the students to become familiar with the beautiful readings from the Book of Isaiah that are proclaimed at liturgy during this season. Divide the following reading from Isaiah 40:3-5 into parts and use it as a classroom prayer.

Reader 1: A voice cries out:
In the desert prepare the way of the LORD!

All: **Make straight in the wasteland a**
highway for our God!

Reader 2: Every valley shall be filled in,
every mountain and hill shall be made low;

All: **The rugged land shall be made a plain,**
the rough country, a broad valley.

Reader 3: Then the glory of the LORD shall be revealed,
and all humankind shall see it together;

All: **For the mouth of the LORD has spoken.**

These words were written to be a source of comfort and hope to the people in exile. This reading brings hope today to people who wait in darkness for the coming of the light of Christ.

Advent Promise

Advent is a time of preparation. It is also a time of promise. We wait in expectation for the coming of Jesus at Christmas.

During the season of Advent we prepare our hearts for Jesus. We think about our lives and how we share Jesus with others. Advent is also a time for renewal of God's Spirit in our lives.

Children should understand these deeper meanings of Advent. They need to do more than decorate homes and classrooms for the coming of Christmas. They also need to prepare their hearts for the coming of Jesus. One way to enable them to do this is with an Advent promise.

Forms for this activity can be duplicated on half sheets of green paper. Put the words "Advent Promise" prominently at the top. Then print the following pledge:

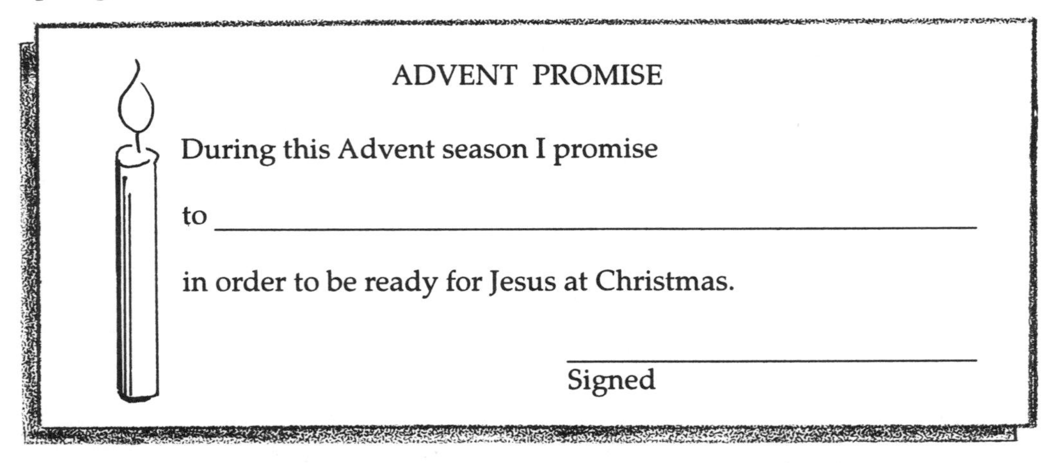

ADVENT PROMISE

During this Advent season I promise

to ______________________________

in order to be ready for Jesus at Christmas.

____

Signed

On the left side of the paper draw a candle as a reminder that we are waiting for the light of Christ to come into our lives.

Discuss with the students various ways that they can display their readiness for Christmas through how they live and how they act. Help them to focus on ways to pray and ways to help other people. The class discussion can help them think of things they might do, but each student should pick something personally meaningful to him or her.

Next, ask them to write their Advent promise on the lines of the form. Remind them that their signature is a pledge to carry out what they have written.

These forms can be presented as part of a class prayer service or liturgy. Encourage the students to share the promise with their families. Making an Advent promise helps students take the love and hope they learn in class to their lives outside the boundaries of the classroom.

Penny Power Project

Many local organizations collect gifts during Advent to distribute to children in need. These organizations rely on contributions from the community to fund their Christmas giving program. A wonderful way for children to help other children during Advent is by contributing pennies. This project could even begin well before Advent. Donate the collected money to one of these organizations in support of their efforts.

Publicity is a must. At the latest, the collection should start at the very beginning of Advent. Send notes to the parents letting them know about this project. Check with the organization to find out their deadline for receiving the donated money.

Children should be encouraged to participate, but not required. Some of their families may be going through hard times themselves or they may choose to contribute to another worthy organization instead.

Brightly-colored collection cans can be made from coffee cans and placed in each classroom with a sign announcing the "Penny Power" project. It is amazing how much money can be collected in pennies. People are usually very willing to donate pennies. Hundreds of pennies do add up! The pennies should be taken to the bank to be counted. A check can then be drawn in the name of the organization and forwarded to them.

Be sure to thank the children and parents for their participation and to let them know how much money was collected. This project is a lesson in what can be accomplished when we all work together in Jesus' name.

Living Advent Wreath

Tell the class that they are to decide on a special act of kindness to enact each week of Advent. The group will meet each week to celebrate their actions with prayer in the form of a living Advent wreath. As members of the living Advent wreath they are to light the word not only with candles, but also through the light of their loving actions.

Provide older students with instructions for becoming a living Advent wreath. This is how they do it: choose four students to hold an Advent candle (three candles are purple and one candle is pink). Choose one student to be the Christ bearer; this student holds a large white candle. All the other students hold smaller white taper candles with cardboard wax holders.

The group stands in a circle to represent the Advent wreath. The four Advent candleholders should be inside the circle equal distances from one another. The Christ bearer stands in the very center with the large white candle. Arrange the group in the same way for each week of Advent. Choose readers for the appropriate parts and conduct each prayer service while the participants stand and hold the candles.

First Week of Advent

Leader: The circle of the Advent wreath, without a beginning or an end, symbolizes God's unending love for us. The evergreen in the traditional wreath represents growth and the hope of eternal life. The four candles stand for the four weeks before Christmas, as well as the thousands of years people waited for the coming of the Messiah.

As we light the candle for the first week of Advent, let us reflect on the birth of Christ. (Christ bearer lights the first purple candle).

All: **The Lord brings the light of PEACE to his people; a light that no darkness of violence or trouble can extinguish.**

Reader 1: The beginning of John's Gospel tells us: "A man named John was sent from God. He came for testimony, to testify to the light, so that all might believe through him. He was not the light, but came to testify to the light. The true light, which enlightens everyone, was coming into the world" (John 1:6-9).

All: **Let us walk in the light of PEACE.**

Reader 2: This week we choose to be a PEACEMAKER in our families by responding kindly and generously when we are asked to do a chore, an errand, or something extra. Think about a way that you will be a peacemaker. (All silently decide on one specific way to be a peacemaker in the coming week. Then each students lights their taper from the Advent candle.)

All: **Let us walk in the light of PEACE.** (Extinguish all candles.)

Second Week of Advent

Leader: The theme of the second week of Advent is preparation. The purple candles of the Advent wreath remind us that Advent is a time for preparation and sacrifice. The lighting of candles each week in Advent marks our growing anticipation of the second coming of Christ, Light of the World.

All: **The Lord brings the light of peace to his people; a light that no darkness of violence or trouble can extinguish. Let us walk in the light of PEACE.** (Christ bearer re-lights the purple candle for the first week of Advent.)

The Lord brings the light of JUSTICE to his people, a light no darkness of prejudice or cruelty can extinguish. (The Christ bearer lights another candle for the second week of Advent.)

Reader 1: Jesus said, "I am the light of the world. Whoever follows me will not walk in darkness, but will have the light of life" (John 8:12).

All: **Let us walk in the light of JUSTICE.**

Reader 2: This week we choose JUSTICE by doing or saying one thing to defend the poor, the downtrodden or the persecuted. Think about a way that you will be a person of justice. (All silently decide on one specific way to practice justice in the coming week. Then each student lights their taper from one of the lighted Advent candles.)

All: **Let us walk in the light of PEACE and JUSTICE.** (Extinguish all candles.)

Third Week of Advent

Leader: During Advent we remember Christ's coming as a baby in Bethlehem. But we also remember that Christ is present with us now. The theme of the third week of Advent is rejoicing. We have a reason to rejoice because God is with us. Throughout the Bible, fire symbolizes the presence of God. As we light the flame of our Advent wreath, we are reminded of the warm and enlightening presence of God. We light the pink candle to represent our joy.

All: **The Lord brings the light of PEACE to his people; a light that no darkness of violence or trouble can extinguish. Let us walk in the light of PEACE**. (The Christ bearer re-lights the candle for the first week of Advent.)

The Lord brings the light of JUSTICE to his people; a light no prejudice or cruelty can extinguish. Let us walk in the light of JUSTICE. (Christ bearer re-lights the candle for the second week of Advent.)

The Lord brings the light of PATIENCE to his people; a light no greed or selfishness can extinguish. (The Christ bearer lights the pink candle, the candle for the third week of Advent.)

Reader 1: Jesus said to his followers: "It was not you who chose me; but I who chose you and appointed you to go forth and bear fruit that will remain, so that whatever you ask the Father in my name he may give to you: This I command you: love one another" (John 15:16-17).

All: **Let us walk in the light of PATIENCE.**

Reader 2: This week we choose to show PATIENCE by doing one act of kindness for someone younger or older than ourselves—a younger brother or sister, an elderly friend, or grandparent. Think about how you will show patience. (All silently decide on one specific way to practice patience in the coming week. Then each student lights their taper from the flame of one of the Advent candles.)

All: **Let us walk in the light of PEACE, JUSTICE, and PATIENCE.** (Extinguish all candles.)

Fourth Week of Advent

Leader: The theme of the fourth week of Advent is HOPE. When all four candles on our Advent wreath are lit we will have a full circle of light. Let us be people of trust and hope. As we light the fourth candle, let us turn our thoughts to Mary, whose trust in the Lord's promise was fulfilled at the birth of Christ.

All: **The Lord brings the light of PEACE to his people; a light that no darkness of violence or trouble can extinguish. Let us walk in the light of PEACE.** (The Christ bearer re-lights the candle for the first week of Advent.)

The Lord brings the light of JUSTICE to his people; a light no darkness of prejudice or cruelty can extinguish. Let us walk in the light of JUSTICE. (The Christ bearer re-lights the candle for the second week of Advent.)

The Lord brings the light of PATIENCE to his people; a light no darkness of greed or selfishness can extinguish. Let us walk in the light of PATIENCE. (The Christ bearer re-lights the pink candle.)

The Lord brings the light of HOPE to his people; a light no darkness of suffering, worry, or fear can extinguish. (The Christ bearer lights the third purple candle.)

Reader 1: Jesus said to his disciples: "Therefore I tell you, do not worry about your life and what you will eat, or about your body and what you will wear . . . . Notice the ravens: they do not sow or reap; they have neither storehouse nor barns, yet God feeds them. How much more important are you than birds? Can any of you by worrying add a moment to your life-span?" (Luke 12:22-25).

Reader 2: Let us choose HOPE by trusting the Lord to answer our prayers to resolve a difficult situation, personal problem, or the need of a family member or friend. Think about how you will choose hope. (All silently decide on one specific need to place in the hands of the Lord with trust and hope. Then each student lights their taper in the flame of one of the Advent candles.)

All: **This week let us walk in the light of PEACE, JUSTICE, PATIENCE, and HOPE.** (Extinguish all candles.)

Mary's Feast Day

December 8 is the feast of the Immaculate Conception. This is the day we celebrate that Mary was without sin from the beginning of her life. It is also appropriate to remember Mary during Advent because she waited in a very special way for Jesus to come. Mary is a model of faithfulness and trust in God.

There are many ways to help children learn about Mary, the Mother of God:

~

pray the Hail Mary together and remind the children that we can ask Mary to pray for us;

~

read the beautiful magnificat in Luke 1:46-50 in which Mary praises God and God's gifts to her;

~

sing a traditional Mary song such as Immaculate Mary or another favorite that many of the children already know;

~

say a decade of the rosary in class with different children leading each prayer;

~

put fresh flowers by a statue of Mary in the church or school building on the feast of the Immaculate Conception;

~

help the children learn the joyful, sorrowful, and glorious mysteries of the rosary;

~

ask older students to put on a short play about Mary for a younger group of children;

~

review events in Mary's life including the annunciation, the birth of Jesus, and Mary by the cross;

~

learn about and possibly tour a local Marian shrine;

~

compose a litany prayer using titles of Mary such as "Queen of Heaven" and "Star of Hope."

~

Activities of this kind help the children see that Mary is an example for us of how we should live our lives.

Tree Calendar

A tree calendar is a colorful craft project for the Advent season. This activity helps young children clearly understand that Advent is the four weeks before Christmas, and that the season is a time of waiting and expectation for Christmas.

Have each child cut out a large green Christmas tree from a standard sheet of construction paper. Young children may need to have a pattern to trace around before they begin cutting. Tell the children to put their names on the back of their tree.

The children decorate one part of the tree each week of Advent. Provide colorful self-stick stickers with Christmas symbols like wreaths, bells, and stars. Self-stick stickers are easy for children to use and look terrific.

The first week of Advent the children put one sticker at the top of the tree. The second week they put two stickers just below the first sticker. During the third week they add three stickers on the next row. For the fourth week of Advent the students put four stickers on the bottom area of the tree.

This calendar idea helps children count the weeks of Advent. The children enjoy working with bright Christmas stickers and they like learning by doing. When they finish, have the students take their tree calendar home to use as a Christmas decoration or to give to their families.

Psalm Verse

The beautiful Psalm 25 is recited at Mass during the Advent season. Verses four and five of Psalm 25 make a good Advent prayer and help children see Advent as a time of waiting. Read these verses to the children:

> Your ways, O Lord, make known to
> me;
> teach me in your paths,
> Guide me in your truth and teach me,
> for you are God my savior.
> and for you I wait all the day.
>
> ~Psalm 25:4-5

Discuss the meaning of these verses with the children. Ask them how these words help to express our longing for God and our desire to be faithful people.

Duplicate the words of the prayer. Fold a piece of blue construction paper in half. Blue is a traditional choice for Advent since it indicates the darkness before the dawn of the light of Christ. Trim and mount the prayer on the inside of the construction paper. This forms a stand-up prayer card.

Repeat the prayer together in class. Then encourage the children to take home their prayer card and pray this prayer each day during the remainder of the Advent season.

Heart Wreath

Advent is a season of love. God has given us a great capacity for sharing the gift of love. Giving presents to others is one way that we do this.

Making and sharing a heart wreath can help the children understand this theme. At the beginning of the Advent season have each child cut out one wreath (8″ diameter) from green construction paper. The edges should be cut in a jagged manner to give the wreath a holly feel.

Next, have each child cut out a paper bow from red construction paper, print their name in the middle of the bow, and glue it to the top of the wreath. Display the wreaths on a classroom wall or bulletin board.

Place a supply of shiny red heart stickers in a basket in a place where the children can reach them. The heart is a universal symbol of love. Tell the children that each time during Advent that they help someone or show care toward another person, they can add a heart sticker to their wreath.

Hopefully by the time Christmas draws near, the wreath will be decorated with many red hearts. The children can take their wreath home and use it as a door decoration.

This idea helps children focus their efforts in Advent on giving to others rather than living in expectation of receiving their own Christmas gifts.

Advent Angels

The Advent angels project is another way to remind children to serve the needs of others. Ask the children to print their names on a piece of paper and put them in a basket. Call one child at a time to draw a name. (If a child draws his or her own name, have them draw again.)

The children act as Advent angels by doing good deeds in secret for the person whose name they have picked. Advent angels do things like:

~

writing a note to a partner commenting about something good
he or she has done;

~

leaving secret treats like candy or a new pencil
at a person's place;

~

praying for the person each day.

~

It's up to the teacher to set reasonable guidelines for this project and see that all children participate.

At an Advent-ending Christmas party the names of the Advent angels are revealed. Arrange for each person to bring a small gift to present to the person who they have been Advent angel for. This project encourages the children to think of what they can do for someone else during the weeks of Advent, and then do it!

Question Chain

A question chain is an activity to help the children count the days until Christmas comes. Duplicate a set of questions for each child. Cut the questions apart so that one question is written on each strip of paper. Purple copy paper adds a seasonal touch to the chain. Here are some questions that can be used for the chain:

Do I share my joy with others?
Can I say "Yes" to God as Mary did?
Have I helped someone today?
Do I hear God calling me?
Do I pray for the needs of others?
Have I said thank you to God for sending Jesus?
Do I trust God?
Do I see God in other people?
Have I asked God for his help today?
Have I followed Jesus today?
Have I shared the good news with others?
Do I praise God and God's goodness?
Do I give of my time to those in need?
Does my life give glory to God?
Do I live as Jesus calls me to?
Do I tell God about the good things that happen to me?
Do I bring happiness to other people?
Do I have faith in God?
Do I help people in need?
Do I call others to Jesus?
Have I prepared my heart for Jesus to come?
Do I share God's love?
Do I bring peace to others?
Do I say I'm sorry to someone I hurt?
Have I thanked God for this day?
Do I let the Holy Spirit work in my life?
Do I live as Jesus taught?
Am I a caring person?
Do I see God's presence in the world?
Do I remember the true meaning of Christmas?

To assemble the chain form the first strip into a link and secure it with tape. Then put the next strip through the link and tape it. This process is repeated until all the strips are linked together.

Have the children take the assembled question chains home. Instruct them to tear off a link of the chain at home each day of Advent and read the question inside. As Christmas draws nearer, the chain get shorter. Hopefully, the questions will inspire the children to reflect on how they should live their lives during the Advent season and beyond.

Give A Gift

Many families do not have the resources to give their children gifts for Christmas. Toys, especially, may be the last item on the family's budget list, well below rent and food.

One way to help these families and children is with the "Give a Gift" campaign. During Advent, begin a campaign to collect new toys for children who wouldn't otherwise receive any Christmas gifts.

This is an excellent service project for children. It helps them learn about the needs of others and the Christian virtue of charity.

Present details of the program to children and their families well before the beginning of Advent. The gifts should be brought in unwrapped so it can be determined what toys have been donated, and for which ages and sexes they would be most appropriate. Also, contact an established community or church-related organization that already has a system of toy distribution to the needy in place. These organizations usually need toy donations by mid-December. Sometimes these organizations sponsor Christmas parties at which the toys are distributed. Check to see if your group can also attend.

The Give a Gift campaign serves two needs: the children receiving the toys have a more joyful Christmas because of this project and the children giving the gifts learn an important Advent lesson.

Advent Prayer Service

Prayer should mark all important occasions; an Advent prayer service can help the children remember what Advent is all about. Choose students for the following parts. Conduct this prayer service in church or create a comfortable setting in class by re-arranging desks and chairs to provide a large open space where the children can gather in a circle in chairs or on the floor.

Opening Song

Come, Lord Jesus (Young People's Glory and Praise)

Greeting

Leader: Come into our hearts, Lord Jesus.

All: **And help us become all that we were created to be.**

Opening Prayer

Leader: Dear God, we gather to celebrate the season of Advent. As we await the coming of Jesus help us remember that this is a time of faith in God, hope for the future, and love for one another.

All: **Amen.**

Bible Reading

Reader: A reading from the gospel of John (1:6-9).

A man named John was sent from God. He came for testimony, to testify to the light, so that all might believe through him. He was not the light, but came to testify to the light. The true light, which enlightens everyone, was coming into the world. The word of the Lord.

All: **Thanks be to God.**

Prayer Response

Reader: May Advent be a time to prepare for the coming of Jesus, we pray . . .

All: **Lord, hear our prayer.**

Reader: May Advent be a time of sharing with those in need, we pray . . .

All: **Lord, hear our prayer.**

Reader: May Advent be a time of prayer and reflection, we pray . . .

All: **Lord, hear our prayer.**

Reader: May Advent be a time of peace and joy, we pray . . .

All: **Lord, hear our prayer.**

Reader: May Advent be a time when we love others as God loves us, we pray . . .

All: **Lord, hear our prayer.**

Closing Prayer

Leader: Dear God, you have heard our prayers. Help us to share what we have with others during this holy season. May we keep our minds and hearts on the coming of your kingdom, now and always.

All: **Amen.**

Leader: May the light of Christ shine in our lives.

All: **Now and forever.**

Closing Song

Celebrate God (Young People's Glory and Praise)

Mosaic Wreath

Children can make mosaic wreaths to decorate their classrooms and homes during Advent.

Cut one wreath (8″ diameter) from posterboard for each child. Next, have the children tear small pieces of green construction paper. The torn pieces do not need to be of uniform size and should be torn rather than cut with a scissors. This helps to produce the mosaic effect. Have the children use a glue stick to glue the paper onto the wreath.

The children should continue tearing and gluing pieces of paper until the posterboard ring is completely covered and a mosaic wreath has been created.

For a final touch, cut bows from red construction paper and have the children glue it to the top. Place a piece of two-sided tape on the back of the wreath. Hang the wreaths where all can see!

Mary Echo Pantomime

An echo pantomime is a great way to help children understand a Bible story. The reading from Luke 1 of the annunciation of Jesus' birth can be retold in this way. The teacher recites each line and demonstrates the motion. The children echo the words and motions line by line.

An angel came to Mary	*(fold hands)*
sent by God.	*(open arms, look up)*
The angel Gabriel said,	*(hands by mouth)*
Hail, Mary, full of grace.	*(bow from waist)*
Mary was afraid,	*(hands cover face)*
but listened to the angel.	*(hand by ear)*
The angel told her,	*(hands by mouth)*
she was to have a baby.	*(rock arms)*
He would be God's son	*(hand on heart)*
and his name would be Jesus.	*(open arms)*
Mary told the angel	*(hands by mouth)*
that she would do God's will.	*(hand on heart)*
Mary went to see Elizabeth	*(walk in place)*
who was her cousin.	*(nod head)*
Elizabeth said to Mary,	*(hands by mouth)*
blessed are you among women.	*(one arm outstretched)*
And Mary said,	*(hands my mouth)*
my soul proclaims the Lord.	*(hands over heart)*
My spirit rejoices;	*(arms outstretched)*
holy is God's name.	*(bow head, fold hands)*
Then Mary went home	*(walk in place)*
To await Jesus' birth.	*(rock arms)*

The echo pantomime helps the children understand and remember the annunciation story.

O Antiphon Prayer

During the final week of Advent the *O Antiphons* are sung at Mass. Beginning on December 17 and continuing until December 23, a different antiphon is sung each day until Christmas. The *O Antiphons* are part of a litany that contains titles of Jesus. They were originally sung in Latin.

The following prayer service can be recited the week before Christmas. It contains the O Antiphons and concludes with the singing of "O Come, O Come, Emmanuel"—the final *O Antiphon.*

Select readers for the various student parts. Briefly practice the verses and the refrain of "O Come, O Come, Emmanuel" before beginning the prayer.

Introduction

Leader: The O Antiphons have been a part of Advent prayer for many years. As we come to the final week of Advent, we express the hope of the season in prayer. We wait for Jesus to come. We call on the name of the Lord.

Intercessions

Reader 1: O Wisdom from all eternity,

All: **Come and teach us your ways.**

Reader 2: O Lord of Israel,

All: **Come and help us to know that you are God.**

Reader 3: O shoot of Jesse,

All: **Come as we wait in joyful hope.**

Reader 4: O key of David,

All: **Come and free us from the wrong we have done.**

Reader 5: O rising dawn,

All: **Come and help us turn toward your light.**

Reader 6 O King of all nations,

All: **Come that we may we live in peace with one another.**

Reader 7: O Emmanuel,

All: **Come and be with us now and forever.**

Closing Song

O Come, O Come, Emmanuel

Chapter 2

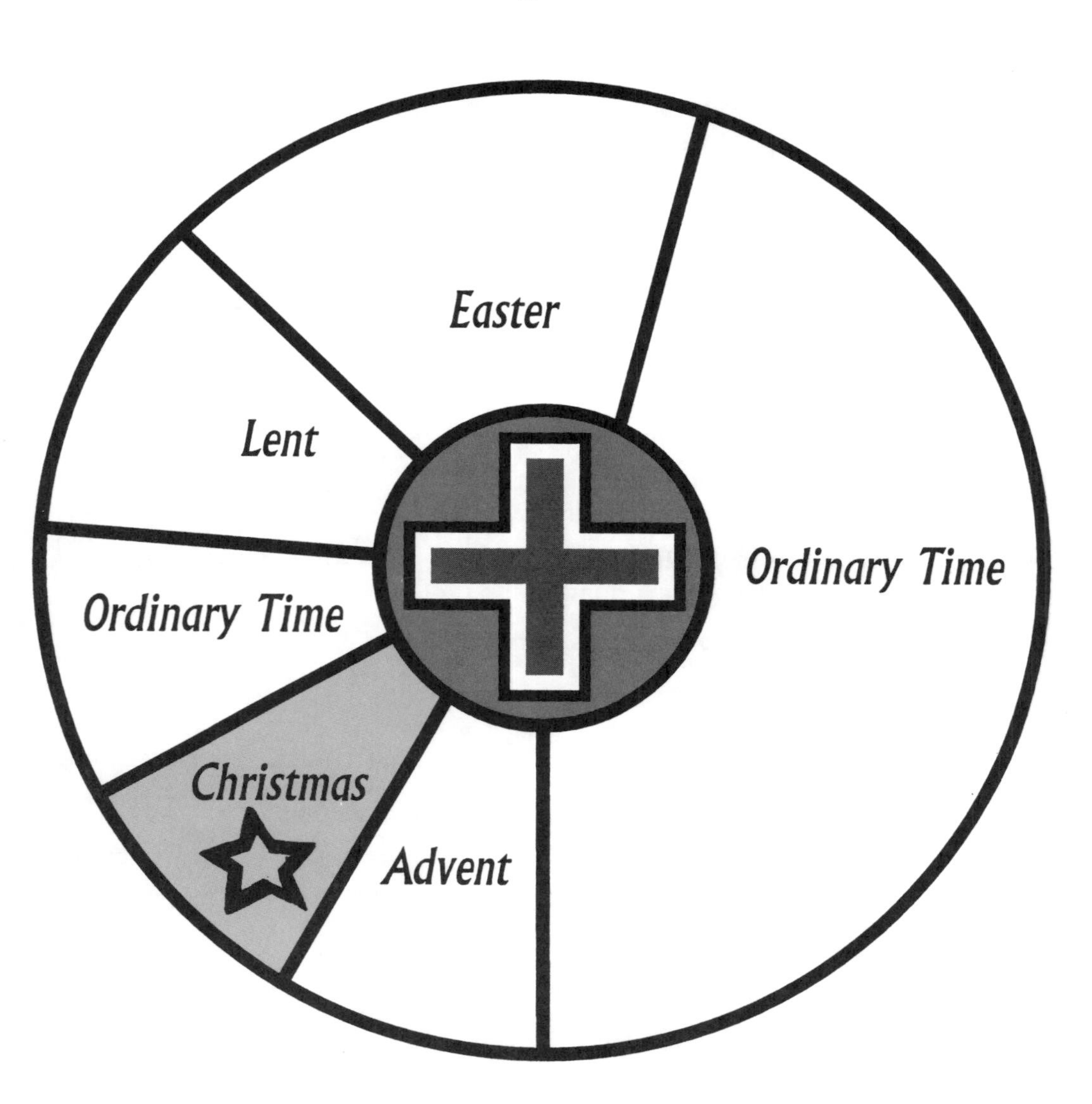

~Christmas~

☆

We Celebrate God's Love

For today in the city of David, a savior has been born
for you who is Messiah and Lord.
~Luke 2:ll~

A new day has dawned for the people of God with the coming of Jesus at Christmas! Jesus shared in our human life so that we could share in the divine life of the Trinity. The birth of the Christ Child in Bethlehem was the beginning of a new dimension in the relationship between God and humankind.

During this season, we celebrate not only the unending love God has for us, but the love we *should have* for others. Christians share the joy of Christmas with other people. We especially reach out to those who are ill, lonely, hungry, homeless, or in need through prayer and service. The Christmas season challenges us to see Christ in others.

In fact, the emphasis of the Christmas season is not so much on the Bethlehem event of 2,000 years ago, but on Christ present here among us today. The nativity event is more than an historical drama that is re-enacted each year. It is a time to reflect on how Jesus comes into our lives daily and for all times to come.

Christmas must make a difference in our lives before it can make a difference in the life of the world. As the angels announced the good news of Christ's birth, so must we live and tell others about the ongoing presence of Jesus Christ for all people.

Joy to the world. The Lord is come!

Manger Prayer

The first crèche, or manger scene, was set up by St. Francis to remind people of the meaning of the Christmas celebration. He used live animals and people to dramatize the birth of Christ.

Today we display crèche scenes in our classrooms, our churches, and our homes for the same purpose. The figures of the Christ Child, Mary, Joseph, animals, and shepherds help us remember the holy day many years before.

Involve the children in setting up a classroom manger scene. Gather the children before the stable and distribute the figures listed in the prayer service below to individual children.

Then, standing before the stable, sing together the opening song. Read the opening prayer. Ask the child with the donkey to read the designated part and to then reverently put the donkey figure in place. The prayer response is said by all. Continue the service in the same manner with the other figures. Read the closing prayer. Conclude with all the children singing "Joy to the World."

Opening Song

O Come All Ye Faithful

Opening Prayer

Leader: Loving Father, we thank you for sending your Son, Jesus, to us on the first Christmas. As we gather today before this manger scene, help us understand more about the true meaning of Christmas. We make this prayer in your name.

All: **Amen.**

Nativity Story

Donkey: This is the donkey that carried Mary many miles from Nazareth to Bethlehem. The donkey and other animals provided warmth in the stable on the night that Jesus was born.

All: **We praise the goodness of your creation.**

Shepherd: This is one of the shepherds who was caring for his sheep that night on the hills outside of Bethlehem. Many shepherds left their watch to see the baby Jesus.

All: **We praise the goodness of all who have come to believe.**

Joseph: This is Mary's husband, Joseph. He helped care for Mary and Jesus on this night and beyond.

All: **We praise the goodness of Joseph, husband of Mary.**

Mary: This is Mary, mother of Jesus, mother of God. She said yes when God asked her to be the mother of his Son.

All: **We praise the goodness of Mary, mother of God, and our mother too.**

Christ Child: This is the Christ Child, the savior of the world. Christmas is the day we remember his birth.

All: **We praise the goodness of the Christ Child, the image of his Father's love.**

Closing Prayer

Leader: Father, at Christmas we clearly see your love for us. Help us to share your love with people in our family, in our community, and in our world. As we welcome Jesus, may we also welcome all people in his name. We ask this in your name.

All: **Amen.**

Closing Song

Joy to the World

Paper Chain

Making a red and green paper chain is a traditional and enjoyable Christmas project. Encourage the children to work together on one very long Christmas chain.

One sheet of red and one sheet of green construction paper (8 1/2" x 11") is needed for each six feet of chain. Cut the paper into approximately 1" x 8 1/2" strips. A paper cutter makes the job fast and easy.

Show the children how to make a paper chain by forming one red strip into a circle and taping or gluing the ends together. Then loop a green strip through the red circle and connect it in the same way. Instruct the children continue to alternate colors until they have made their own chain.

Next, have the children connect their chains together until one long chain is formed.

The chain can be used to trim the classroom Christmas tree or hung in swags across the top of the chalkboard. This is also an inexpensive way to decorate a stage area for a Christmas production or the cafeteria for a Christmas party.

This project also helps children learn what they can accomplish when they all work together. The red and green chain looks festive and adds a splash of Christmas color to the children's area.

Christmas Beatitudes

A popular saying reminds us that "Jesus is the reason for the season." The following Christmas beatitudes meditation can help us to keep Christ in Christmas. Everyone can participate by saying the response; several students can read the other sections.

Reader 1: Blessed are they who find Christmas in the fragrant greens, the cheerful holly, and the soft flicker of candles.

All: **To them shall come bright memories of love and happiness.**

Reader 2: Blessed are they who find Christmas in the Christmas star.

All: **May their lives ever reflect its beauty and its light.**

Reader 3: Blessed are they who find Christmas in the happy music of the Christmas season.

All: **A song of joy will sing forever in their hearts.**

Reader 4: Blessed are they who find Christmas in the age old story of a baby born in a stable.

All: **For them a little child will always mean hope and promise in a troubled world.**

Reader 5: Blessed are they who find Christmas in the coming of the Prince of Peace.

All: **Help them to share his peace on earth and his good will to all.**

Encourage the children to write their own Christmas beatitudes which tell ways they experience Christ's presence in this season.

Adopt-a-Family

Adopt-a-family is a service project that benefits families in need. Children and adults alike collect Christmas gifts and food items for parish or community families who need holiday assistance.

Publicize the project in the parish bulletin, and program newsletter. Provide the phone number of the project coordinator or parish social ministry director. The coordinator records information about the families who request assistance: the number of people in the family, the ages and sizes of the children, special requests, address, and phone number.

The coordinator is the only person who knows the names of the families. Each family's wish list of requests should be typed and referred to by a letter or number designation.

Each class is responsible for buying one item for the basket. The gifts should be wrapped and marked on the outside with a designation such as "girl, age 3".

Put the food items in a decorative holiday basket. Include things like cans or boxes of vegetables, stuffing, gravy, potatoes, fruit, and other nonperishable items. If your group is providing turkeys, make sure they remain frozen until it is time for delivering. Adding a box of Christmas candy is also a nice touch.

The project coordinator and/or designated adult volunteers personally deliver the items. The adopt-a-family project is a great way for children to really help those who need a share of good will during the holiday season.

Sticker Prayer

Children enjoy using stickers on projects. Use colorful stickers to help the children illustrate a Christmas prayer. The following prayer can be printed on paper by the children or duplicated for them before class:

~A Christmas Prayer~

For the gift of music and carols,
thank you God.
For the gift of trees and wreaths,
thank you God.
For the gift of one another,
thank you God.
For the gift of your love,
thank you God.
For the gift of your Son, Jesus,
thank you God.
For the gift of Christmas,
thank you God.

Have the children add appropriate Christmas stickers to each verse. For example one sticker could be placed to the right of the first verse, a second sticker to the left of the second verse, and so on.

Have the children glue the decorated prayer onto a green sheet of construction paper to form the appearance of a frame. Encourage the children to post their Christmas sticker prayer at home and to pray it together with their families.

Greeting Card

Ask the children to make a Christmas greeting card for someone special. Explain that this is a great way to express love and attention for another.

Have the children fold in half a light-colored, heavy stock sheet of paper. Provide markers and tell the children use their creativity and draw a picture on the front of the card. For example, they may draw a nativity scene, a Christmas symbol, or a winter scene. If possible, provide craft supplies like glitter and self-stick stars to add to the decoration.

Next, have the children write a personal Christmas greeting on the inside of the card. Remind the students to sign their names! The children can arrange delivery themselves.

Each card is as unique as its designer. This project helps children learn that giving is a message of the season. Christmas cards are a joy to create and a joy to receive.

Hall Mural

Making a class hall mural is an activity that involves all the children in a class. Use a roll of 36"-wide paper. The length of the mural depends on the number of children in the class and the display space available. In the middle of the paper print in large letters using a red marker the words "Merry Christmas".

Spread the mural out on the floor. Invite each student to draw his or her own Christmas decoration, message, or prayer on the mural. The students can all work at the same time by sharing space and markers. However, make sure that the students work from the same side of the mural so that all the decorations face the same way.

The mural will be a great Christmas greeting to all who pass by it and the children will be pleased with their contribution.

Christmas Meditation

Read this adapted version of St. Luke's Christmas story to help the children reflect on the meaning of the birth of Jesus. The meditation can be enhanced by playing an instrumental version of "Silent Night" as background music. Allow a verse of the song to play before beginning the following reading:

> The sun was dawning as Mary and Joseph started out on their long journey. They were going to Bethlehem to register for the census. Mile after mile they traveled. At last, on the second day, they saw Bethlehem in the distance.
>
> The town was very crowded. People were everywhere and there was much confusion. Mary and Joseph went to the inn, but there was no room for them. Joseph told the innkeeper that his wife was soon to have a baby. The innkeeper let them sleep in a cave behind the inn where the animals stayed. That night, in the quiet of the stable, Jesus was born. Mary wrapped him in swaddling clothes and laid him tenderly in a manger of hay.
>
> On the hill outside of town, shepherds watched their sheep as the rest of the town slept. In the darkness of the night the only light was from the galaxy filled with stars. Suddenly a bright light appeared. It was an angel sent from God. The shepherds were afraid, but the angel told them the good news. This very night, the angel said, in a cave in Bethlehem, a savior had been born for all people.
>
> Some of the shepherds went down to the stable. There they found Mary, Joseph, and the baby as the angel had said. The shepherds looked in awe at the sleeping child. Joyfully they praised God for sending Jesus for all people. Today, we likewise thank God for the gift of his Son at Christmas.

This meditation helps the children look anew at the story of the first Christmas. It helps them understand and experience the events of the Christmas story and speaks to them of God's love.

Tree Ornaments

Colorful ornaments can be made for the classroom Christmas tree by using old Christmas cards. Arrange for a collection of old Christmas cards at the end of the Christmas season and save them until next year. Or, purchase old sets from flea markets, garage sales, or bargain stores.

Allow the children to choose the cards they like. Have them cut out the picture on the card into Christmas ornament shapes like stars, stockings, trees, bells, angels, or wreaths. If needed, duplicate ornament patterns for the children to use. Each child should cut out several ornaments.

Punch a hole in the top of each ornament and insert and tie a length of green or red yarn through it. The yarn serves as a hanger for the ornament.

When finished, play a recording of Christmas carols and have the children work together to decorate the classroom tree. This is an inexpensive method of decorating and the colorful cards make bright and attractive tree ornaments.

Psalm 96 Prayer

Psalm 96 from the Christmas midnight Mass can be used by the students as a class prayer. This psalm reminds us that Jesus came for all people.

Everyone is involved in proclaiming the psalm. The left side of the classroom reads the parts marked left, and the right side reads the parts marked right:

Left: Sing to the LORD a new song;
sing to the LORD, all you lands.

Right: Sing to the LORD; bless his name;
announce his salvation, day after day.

Left: Tell his glory among the nations;
among all peoples, his wondrous deeds.

Right: For great is the LORD and highly to be praised;
awesome is he, beyond all gods.

Left: For all gods of the nations are things of nought,
but the LORD made the heavens.

Right: Splendor and majesty go before him;
praise and grandeur are in his sanctuary.

Left: Give to the LORD, you families of nations,
give to the LORD glory and praise.

Right: Give to the LORD the glory due his name!
Bring gifts and enter his courts;

Left: Worship the LORD in holy attire.
Tremble before him all the earth.

Right: Say among the nations: The LORD is king.
He has made the world firm, not to be moved. . .

Left: Let the heavens be glad and the earth rejoice;
Let the sea and what fills it resound;

Right: Let the plains be joyful and all that is in them.
Then shall all the trees of the forest exult.

All: **Before the LORD, for he comes;**
for he comes to rule the earth.
He shall rule the world with justice
and the peoples with his constancy.

This is a joyful psalm that helps us reflect on and express the glory of God.

Class Card

A class card is a simple way to send Christmas greetings from a large group to the pastor or another special recipient.

This project is most easily done with a computer. Use a graphics program to print a large Christmas symbol in the center of a standard sheet of paper. Also, put a border around the page. Then, in large type print the words "Merry Christmas" with the first word, Merry, over the graphic and the second word, Christmas, under the graphic. Print or copy the page on colorful sheets of red and green paper to enhance the look.

Have each student in the class sign his or her name and write a short message on the page. The teacher should also sign the greeting and indicate the grade level or room number. Create separate pages for more than one class. Vary the symbol, border, greeting, and paper color so that each class card has a different look. Fasten all the pages together to form one book.

Present the class card to the recipient before Christmas. It is a very special gift indeed to receive greetings signed by everyone in a school or religious education program.

Joy Banner

A joy banner can be made from materials readily available in the classroom to help children express what the Christmas season is about.

First, have the children cut a piece of 8 1/2″ x 11″ green construction paper in half lengthwise. A half-sheet is just the right size for this banner. Next, distribute a 2′ piece of green yarn to each person. Show them how to fold the top inch of the smaller side of the paper over the yarn, tape the paper in place, and tie the ends of the yarn together to form a loop for hanging.

Then, give each child a piece of red construction paper, about 3″x 9″. On the extra half sheet of green paper, have them print J-O-Y in block letters, cut them out, and glue them vertically to the red paper. Finally, have them center and glue the red paper to the green banner.

The children can hang their paper banner on a doorknob to express Christmas joy to others.

Action Song

Young children enjoy singing traditional Christmas carols with actions that help dramatize the words. The following are simple actions to accompany the words of "Away in the Manger." Demonstrate the actions as you sing along with the children.

~Verse 1~

Away in a manger No crib for a bed.	*(rock arms)*
The little Lord Jesus Laid down his sweet head.	*(hands by head)*
The stars in the sky Look down where he lay.	*(point up)*
The little Lord Jesus Asleep on the hay.	*(rock arms)*

~Verse 2~

The cattle are lowing, the poor Baby wakes,	*(hands by mouth)*
But little Lord Jesus, No crying he makes;	*(finger on mouth)*
I love you, Lord Jesus. Look down from the sky,	*(hand on heart)*
And stay by my cradle Till morning is nigh.	*(rock arms)*

This song can be sung in the classroom or performed in a Christmas program. The actions help young children understand that at Christmas we celebrate the birth of Jesus.

Nativity Wreath

A nativity wreath provides a visual reminder of why we celebrate Christmas.

Provide one sheet of green construction paper to each child and have them cut out a wreath. The children can trace the outer and inner circles of the wreath using two different sizes of heavy paper plates.

Make copies of nativity figures—Mary, Joseph, the Christ Child, a manger, a sheep, and a star—for each child from a reproducible coloring book. Have the children color these figures with crayons. Then, have them carefully cut out the individual figures and glue them to the wreath. The Christ Child in the manger should be placed at the bottom. The other figures can be filled-in proportionately on each side. The star goes at the top.

The nativity wreath tells the Christmas story without using words. It is a terrific way to help children understand and celebrate Christmas.

Shelter Project

As Mary and Joseph were once turned away from the inn because there was no room for them, many families today are turned away from homeless shelters because there are not enough beds to go around.

Help the students become aware of the needs of homeless people in their own communities. The problem of homelessness is widespread. Most shelters depend on private donations for a majority of their operating budget.

A worthwhile Christmas service project is to collect money from students, parents, and teachers and donate the collection to a local homeless shelter. Inquire at the local night shelter about the per-day cost for one person. Make this amount your minimum goal. The cost-per-day figure usually includes three meals, shelter, and other services. Shelters also offer additional services including counseling, employment referral, and educational opportunities.

Deliver your donation before Christmas. Also, encourage the children to pray for the needs of homeless people and to especially remember them in prayer on Christmas day.

Christmas Bookmark

Making bible bookmarks for Christmas is an ideal project for younger children. Distribute one 2″ x 6″ piece of green posterboard to each child. Have them use a red marker to print a greeting like "Merry Christmas" across the length of one side. Have them save room for a sticker at the end of the greeting. Then, on the other side have the children print an appropriate Christmas Bible verse with reference. For example:

Glory to God in the highest.	*Luke 2:14*
She gave birth to her firstborn son.	*Luke 2:6*
I proclaim to you good news.	*Luke 2:10*
A savior has been born.	*Luke 2:11*

To make the bookmarks durable, cover them front and back with clear, self-adhesive book covering.

Encourage the children to take their bookmarks home and place them in the family bible to mark the location of the Christmas story. They will know where to put the bookmark by looking at the scripture reference printed on it.

On Christmas day the children can request a family member to read the entire Christmas story out loud for all to hear.

Candle Craft

Making candles is a great Christmas craft. Children really enjoy this project and are very pleased with how the candles with glitter turn out.

Each child needs a baby food jar. A notice in the parish bulletin usually brings in more than enough jars.

Have the children apply white glue to the outside of the jar with a paint brush. Put glitter in a bowl and let the children roll the jars in the bowl. They like this part the best!

Allow time for the glue to dry. Give each child a small votive candle to put inside the decorated jar. When you light the candles, the colors of the glitter will be illuminated. Dim the lights and use the glitter candles as part of a class prayer service.

Tell the children that they can take their candles home but that the candles are to only be lit by an adult. Suggest that the candle be displayed on the dinner table and lit every time the family prays during the Christmas season.

Christmas Story Prayer Service

A class prayer service at Christmas time helps students focus on the birth of Jesus. The following prayer service provides an opportunity for all the students to participate. Choose readers for the various parts. Also, you may wish to assign seasonal pictures that all the children can draw to be hung on the walls in the prayer service area.

Opening Song

Silent Night

Greeting

Leader: As Christmas draws near, we pause to reflect on the true meaning of this wonderful season. The first Christmas happened because God loved us so much that he sent the world his only Son, Jesus.

All: **Amen.**

Bible Reading

Narrator: The Christmas story according to the Gospel of Luke. In those days a decree went out from Caesar Augustus that the whole world should be counted in a census.

Joseph: And Joseph too went up from Galilee from the town of Nazareth to the city of David, called Bethlehem, because he was of the house and family of David, to be enrolled with Mary his betrothed, who was with child.

Mary: While they were there, the time came for her to have her child and she gave birth to her firstborn son. She wrapped him in swaddling clothes and laid him in a manger, because there was no room for them in the inn.

Shepherd: Now there were shepherds in that region living in the fields and keeping night watch over their flock. The angel of the Lord appeared to them and the glory of the Lord shone around them, and they were struck with great fear.

Angel: The angel said to them, "Do not be afraid; for behold, I proclaim to you good news of great joy that will be for all people. For today in the city of David a savior has been born for you who is Messiah and Lord. And this will be a sign for you: you will find an infant wrapped in swaddling clothes and lying in a manger. And suddenly there was a multitude of heavenly host with the angel, praising God and saying: "Glory to God in the highest and on earth peace to those on whom his favor rests."

Shepherd: When the angels went away from them to heaven, the shepherds said to one another, "Let's go, then, to Bethlehem to see this thing that has taken place which the Lord has made known to us." So they went in haste and found Mary and Joseph, and the infant lying in the manger. When they saw this, they made known the message that had been told them about this child. All who heard it were amazed by what had been told them by the shepherds.

Mary: And Mary kept all these things. . . in her heart.

Shepherd: Then the shepherds returned glorifying and praising God for all they had heard and seen.

Narrator: The word of the Lord.

All: **Thanks be to God.**

Prayer Response

Reader: Help us to say yes to God's call in our lives as did Mary,

All: **Glory to God in the highest.**

Reader: Help us to faithfully follow God's plan as did Joseph,

All: **Glory to God in the highest.**

Reader: Help us to tell the good news to others as did the angels,

All: **Glory to God in the highest.**

Reader: Help us to honor Jesus as did the shepherds,

All: **Glory to God in the highest.**

Reader: Help us to serve others as Jesus showed us,

All: **Glory to God in the highest.**

Closing Prayer

Leader: Dear God, we thank you for sending Jesus to us. He is the best Christmas gift of all. Help us to share the joy and love of the Christmas season with others. We pray this in the name of your Son, Jesus Christ.

All: **Amen.**

Closing Song

Hark the Herald Angels Sing

Holy Family Prayer

The feast of the Holy Family is celebrated during the Christmas season on December 28. Choose readers for the various petitions. Recite this prayer with your students in honor of this feast day.

Reader 1: For all parents and guardians who love and care for children, we pray to the Lord.

Response: **Lord, hear our prayer.**

Reader 2: For grandparents, aunts, uncles, and other relatives who support family members in many ways, we pray to the Lord.

Response: **Lord, hear our prayer.**

Reader 3: For children who strive to live as God calls us, we pray to the Lord.

Response: **Lord, hear our prayer.**

Reader 4: For families who are struggling with difficult situations, we pray to the Lord.

Response: **Lord, hear our prayer.**

Reader 5: For those who minister to families and their needs, we pray to the Lord.

Response: **Lord, hear our prayer.**

Reader 6: For all families that they may love one another in imitation of the example of the Holy Family, we pray to the Lord.

Response: **Lord, hear our prayer.**

Epiphany Story

Epiphany is a feast that celebrates in a special way Jesus' coming to the world for all people and all nations. Choose five children to read the story of Epiphany from Matthew 2:1-12 as follows. Instruct the rest of the group to respond to each reader with "Come, let us adore him."

Reader 1: When Jesus was born in Bethlehem of Judea, in the days of King Herod, behold magi from the east arrived in Jerusalem saying, "Where is the newborn king of the Jews? We saw his star at its rising and have come to do him homage."

Response: **Come, let us adore him.**

Reader 2: When King Herod heard this, he was greatly troubled, and all Jerusalem with him. Assembling all the chief priests and the scribes of the people, he inquired of them where the Messiah was to be born. They said to him, "In Bethlehem of Judea, for thus it has been written."

Response: **Come, let us adore him.**

Reader 3: After their audience with the king the magi set out. And behold, the star that they had seen at its rising preceded them, until it came and stopped over the place where the child was.

Response: **Come, let us adore him.**

Reader 4: They were overjoyed at seeing the star, and on entering the house they saw the child with his mother Mary. They prostrated themselves and did him homage.

Response: **Come, let us adore him.**

Reader 5: Then they opened their treasures and offered him gifts of gold, frankincense, and myrrh. And having been warned in a dream not to return to Herod, they departed for their country by another way.

Response: **Come, let us adore him.**

This prayer response helps the children learn the story of Epiphany directly from scripture.

Gifts of Love

As part of a lesson on the Epiphany, talk with the children about giving gifts from the heart. The following questions can help with a class discussion. Expand on each of the children's responses.

What are some gifts God gives us?

~love~
~his Son, Jesus~
~the world~
~animals~
~sunshine~
~people~
~life~

What are some gifts we can give God?

~love~
~prayers of praise~
~help for others~
~respect for all people~
~care of our world~

What are some gifts we can give others?

~love~
~time shared with a younger brother or sister~
~a letter to grandparents~
~an assist to a neighbor~
~food to the hungry~
~money to the missions~
~prayer for the needs of others~

God calls us to love. We can give gifts of ourselves. We can give gifts to God from our hearts as the wise men did.

Epiphany Banner

One way to teach the children about Epiphany is to have them make banners featuring wise men following the Christmas star.

The banners can be made from beige burlap (available at fabric and craft stores by the yard). Cut the burlap in individual 8 1/2" x 11" pieces and ask a parent or aide to sew a one inch rod pocket seam at the top of one width before class.

Make the three wise men figures by cutting out a felt triangle for each body and a felt circle for each head. Each wise man figure should be a different color. Use a gold felt star-shape to represent the bright Christmas star.

Have the children arrange all the felt pieces on the burlap before gluing. Also, make sure they put paper underneath the banner to prevent the glue from soaking through to the table.

Finally, have the children put a 9" wooden dowel through the top rod pocket. Tie a piece of blue yarn to both ends of the dowel to form a hanger. The final results are bright, colorful banners that speak of the meaning of Epiphany.

Three Kings Song

Children are able to learn important lessons through singing. A song to teach about the feast of Epiphany can be sung to the familiar tune of "Three Blind Mice." Teach the children the lyrics and have them sing it together.

Three wise kings, three wise kings
Followed the star, followed the star.
They saw it in the sky so bright
And followed it through the day and night
To find the Lord Jesus who is our light.
The three wise kings.

Three wise kings, three wise kings
Followed the star, followed the star.
They came from far away to see
The child Jesus born for you and me
And worship our Lord in harmony.
The three wise kings.

Three wise kings, three wise kings
Followed the star, followed the star.
They traveled on through forest and glen
and found the Lord Jesus to honor him.
They gave him gifts, what a journey it'd been
For three wise kings.

Class Party

Epiphany can be a great time for a class party. Parties are a sign to children that something special is happening.

Have the children make crowns to wear for the party. Crowns symbolize that we are all wise people when we seek Jesus Christ in our lives. Cut 8 1/2" x 14" pieces of yellow construction paper in half lengthwise to make two crowns. Cut sharp points for the crown shape and tape the ends to fit the size of the child's head.

Keep the classroom Christmas decorations and the crèche in place for the party. Set the mood by reading the story of the magi from Matthew 2:1-12.

Feature a singing of the traditional carol "We Three Kings of Orient Are" as the children march around the room or the building wearing their crowns. Choose one student to hold a cardboard star on a stick and lead the procession.

Of course a party is not complete without refreshments. Serve star-shaped cookies with punch. An Epiphany party helps the children to celebrate the joy of Jesus' birth much like his first visitors did.

Glitter Star

To celebrate the Epiphany story have the children make beautiful glitter stars. Cut large sheets of white posterboard into 12″ squares before the children arrive. Using a pattern, have each child cut out a star from his or her piece. There can be many different shapes of stars.

Next, have the children decorate their stars using multi-color glitter. Purchase glitter containers with perforated lids for this project.

Demonstrate how to make a thin ribbon of glue in a swirl design on the star. The glue should not be too thick. Watch to make sure the children do not squeeze out too much at one time.

Then pass around a shirt box and the glitter. Tell each child to place the star in the box and sprinkle on the glitter until the glue is covered. Putting the star in a box makes cleanup easy and keeps the glitter off desks and floor. The leftover glitter can be reused.

These finished glitter stars can be displayed in the classroom in many ways. The stars can be pinned to the bulletin board, used as wall decorations with double-stick tape, or hung from the ceiling. They remind the children that Jesus is the light of our lives.

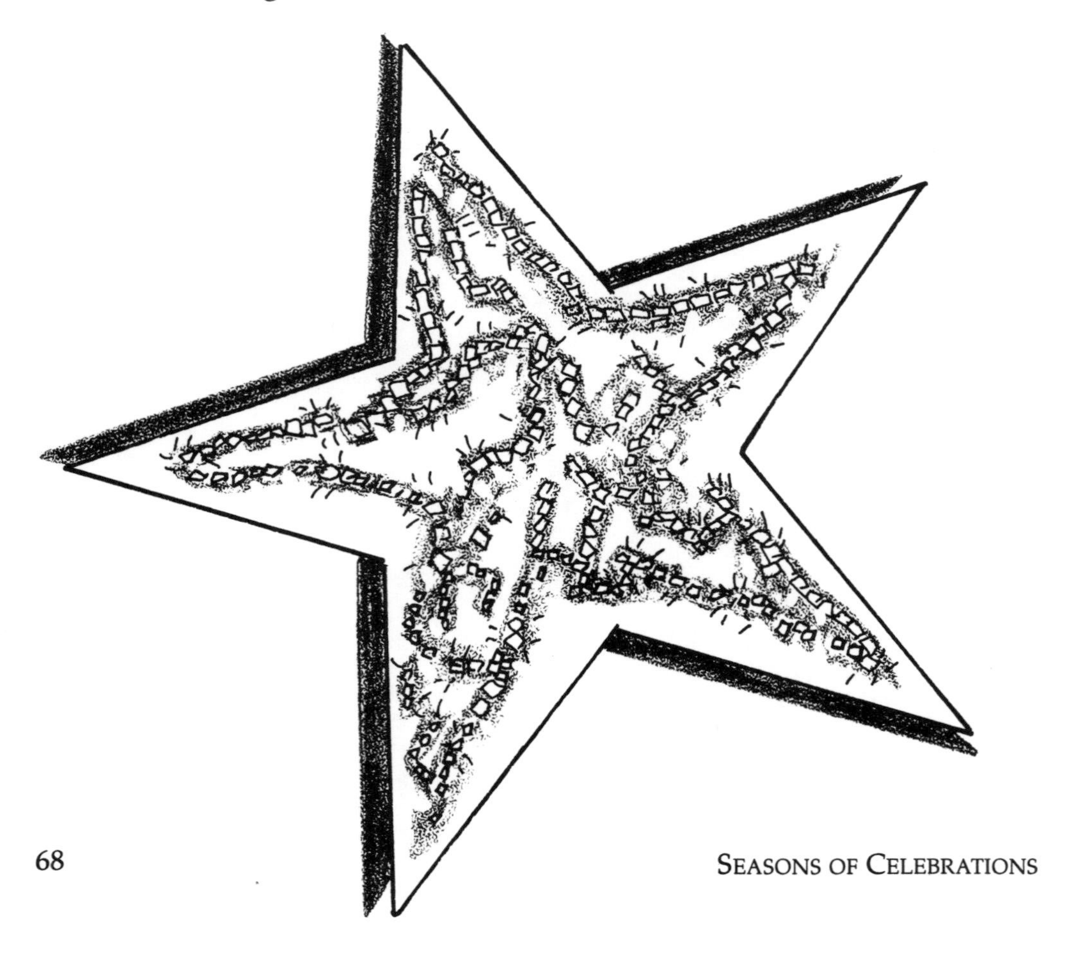

World Prayer

The wise men came from far away to seek Jesus. Epiphany is a time of prayer for world peace. Recite this prayer for peace with your students.

God, Father of us all,
you created the world
and all people in it.

Enable us to live in peace
with all people, all cultures,
all nations.

Help us to remember
that each of us is created
in your image and likeness.

May we focus not on what divides us,
but what unites us—
your love.

Help us to live as your people,
your family,
your children.

We pray this through your Son, Jesus Christ,
who came into the world
that all of us might have life with you.
Amen.

It is important for students to pray together. This prayer helps students remember that we are all God's children.

Chapter 3

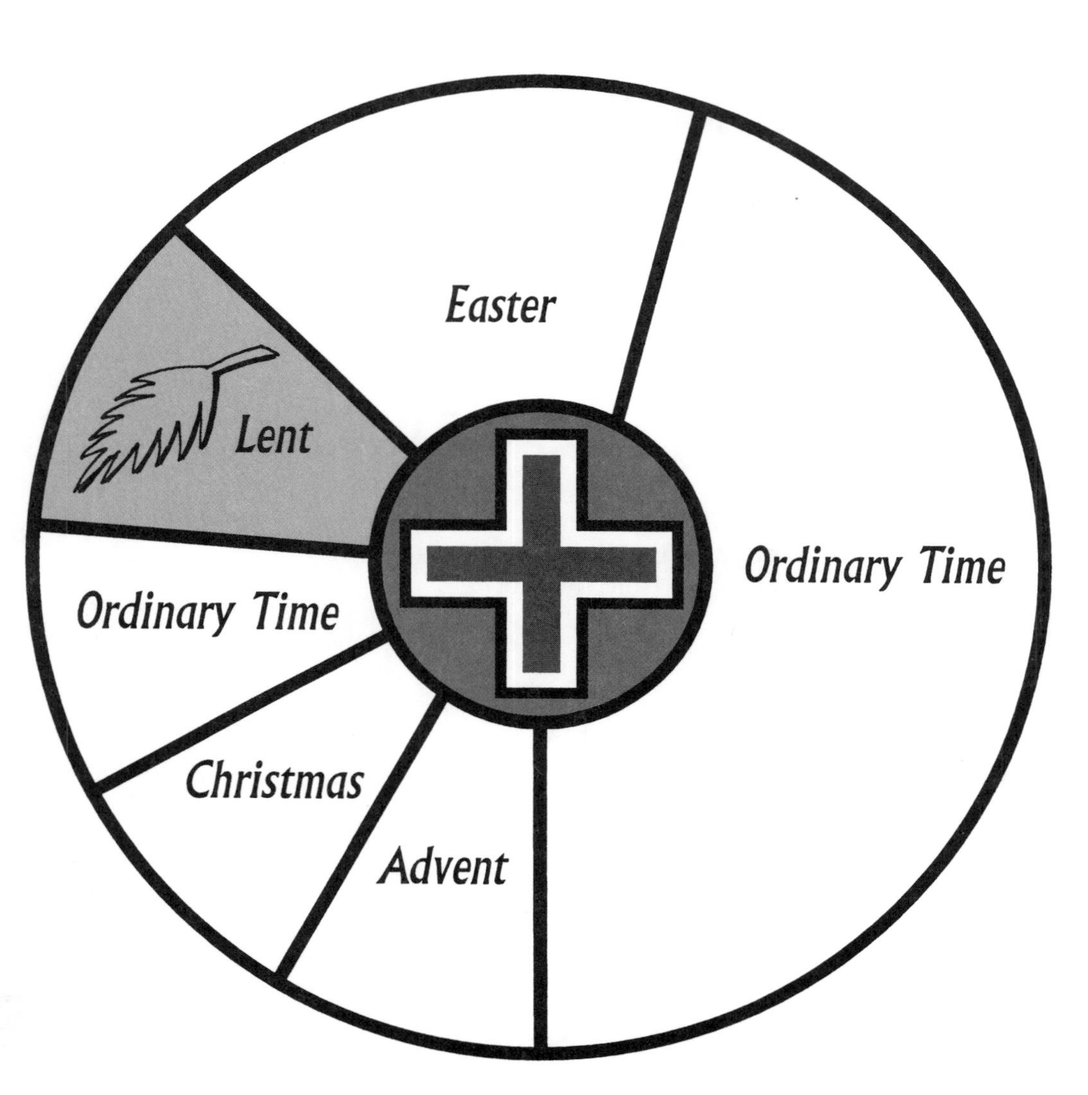

You shall love the Lord your God with all your heart . . .
you shall love your neighbor as yourself.
~Mark 12:30-31~

Lent is a journey of faith. During the time from Ash Wednesday to Holy Thursday we take special care to follow God's will for our lives.

Lent is a time of reconciliation. We ask God's forgiveness and seek to follow Jesus Christ in all things.

Lent is a challenge and call to conversion. During these forty days we prepare to renew and personalize our baptismal commitment. It is a time to move forward toward the light of Easter and the light of Christ in our lives.

Lent is a time to practice living the gospel message by loving God and loving others. During this season we listen carefully to the word of God and reflect on its meaning for our lives. Lent is a time of prayer.

Lent is a time of service. We reach out and help others. We share the love of God with others, especially those with special needs.

In addition to the Lenten activities, this chapter also includes activity and project ideas for the Triduum. The Triduum is actually a separate season between Lent and Easter. During these three days from the Mass of the Lord's Supper on Holy Thursday through Easter Sunday we celebrate the most sacred mysteries of our faith. The word Triduum means three days. During these three days we share not only in Jesus' passion and death, but also in his glorious resurrection.

Ash Wednesday

Traditionally there have been three themes of Lenten observance: prayer, fasting, and almsgiving. To help the children understand these themes, write them on the chalkboard. Use the following discussion ideas to help explain each theme. Print the children's ideas in a column under each topic as they are offered.

Prayer

Through prayer we encounter God in our lives. We pray not only for our needs, but the needs of others. Discuss with the children specific ways we can pray during Lent, including:

—saying the morning offering each day
—thanking God for the many gifts in creation
—praying the stations of the cross with our families
—saying an act of sorrow
—praying for victims of crime, poverty, war, and natural disasters that are in the news
—asking for help to be like Jesus.

Fasting

Fasting helps us to turn away from selfishness toward the light of Christ. We give up something so that others will have more. We fast in order to remind ourselves to change our lives in positive ways. Ask the children to add to the list of "fasting" ideas like the following:

—watching one less television show per week and using the free time to spend with a younger child
—exchanging complaining comments for words of praise
—eating less candy bars and contributing the money saved to an organization that helps the hungry
—stopping unnecessary arguments and acting as a peacemaker instead.

Almsgiving

The gospels list many examples of Jesus' helping others. As Christians, we too are to give of our time, talents, and resources so that others can live better. Discuss with the children many ways to help others, such as:

—donating food to a can drive
—giving away outgrown clothing and toys
—showing compassion to someone who is hurting
—assisting a neighbor with yard work

—welcoming a new student to school
—donating money to an organization that benefits children
—planning and completing a group service project.

Through prayer, fasting, and almsgiving the children can put into practice the spirit of the Lenten season.

Cross Poster

A Lenten cross poster can remind the class that Lent is a time to follow Jesus "on the way to the cross".

Cut a large cross, 22" x 28", from a white sheet of poster board. Use thick marker to print the words "I am the way and the truth and the life" (John 14:6) on the center of the cross.

Discuss with the class the meaning of these words. Stress that Lent is a time to follow Jesus in all we do. Have the students suggest practical ways they can do this: for example, ways to help others and occasions to pray for the needs of others.

After the discussion, have the students cut small crosses (approximately 4 1/2" tall) from purple construction paper. (If you have more than twenty students in class, the crosses should be even smaller.) Tell the students to put their name on their purple cross and glue it to the large white cross.

Display the project in the classroom. The individual purple crosses remind the students to unite their Lenten efforts with the cross of Christ.

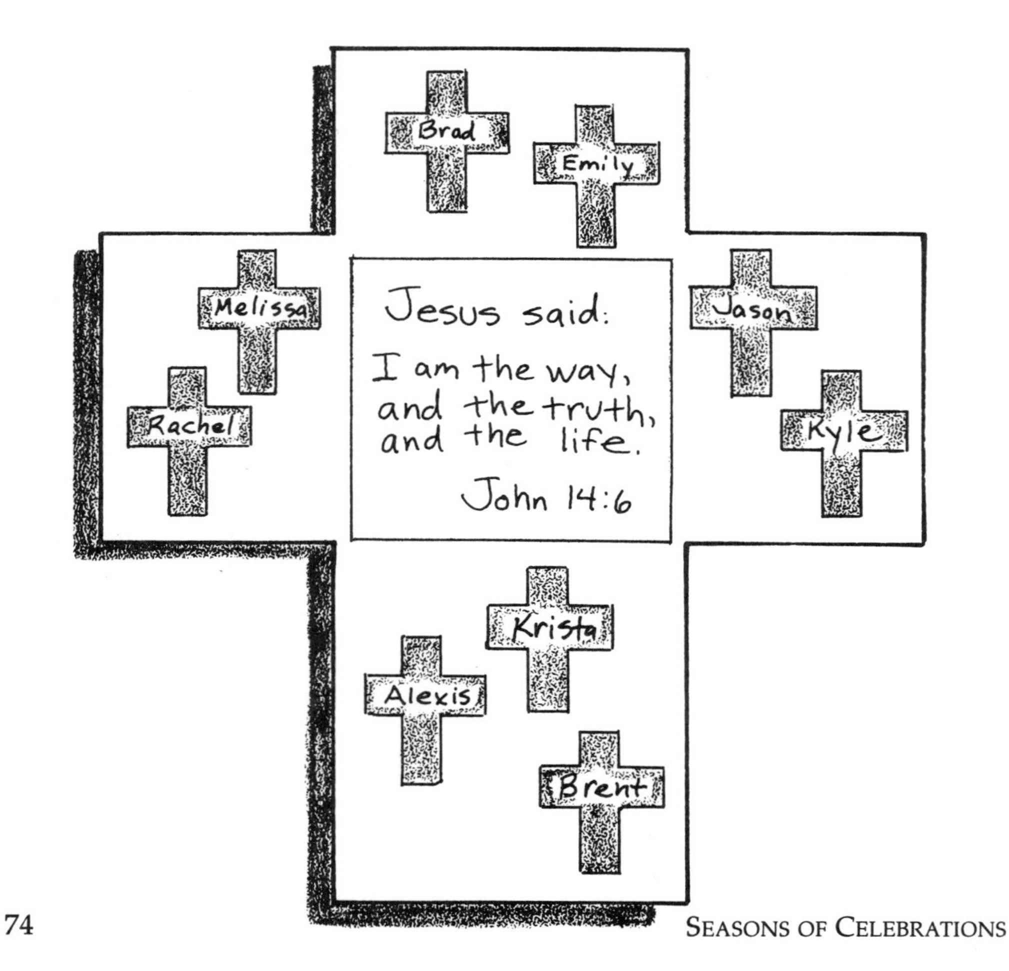

Classroom Calendar

A Lenten calendar is a classroom reminder to help the children live the spirit of the season each day.

Make a large calendar with all the days from Ash Wednesday to Easter Sunday. Print "Lent" across the top. Place that calendar on a bulletin board. Put forty small gold cross stickers in a basket near the calendar. Beginning on Ash Wednesday, ask one child to put a cross on that day's square. Repeat the process with a different child each day. Explain that since each Sunday is a remembrance of Easter, Sundays during Lent are not marked with a cross.

Make the calendar exercise a part of other classroom routines you assign at the beginning of a class period. For example, after the calendar is brought up-to-date, proceed with the opening prayer.

The posted classroom calendar helps give children a sense of the entire Lenten season as they focus on their daily tasks. It serves as a reminder to continue the prayers and good works they have pledged throughout the entire season.

Lent

SUNDAY	MONDAY	TUESDAY	WEDNESDAY	THURSDAY	FRIDAY	SATURDAY
			ASH WED.			
1ST SUNDAY OF LENT						
2ND SUNDAY OF LENT						
3RD SUNDAY OF LENT						
4TH SUNDAY OF LENT						
5TH SUNDAY OF LENT						
PASSION SUNDAY				HOLY THURSDAY	GOOD FRIDAY	EASTER VIGIL
EASTER SUNDAY						

Lent Service Project

Assisting the Holy Childhood Association is a good way for children to help others during Lent. This association has been aiding children in developing nations for over one hundred years. Monetary donations help provide food, shelter, blankets, medicine, health care, education, and other basic necessities to the poorest of the poor.

Explain the project and enlist the cooperation of the students. Encourage the children to donate part of their allowance each week or to do chores at home or in the neighborhood to raise money. Contact the Holy Childhood Association to provide Lent offering boxes for each child.

Collect the offering boxes during Holy Week. Count the money and forward it to the Holy Childhood Association in the form of a check. Report to the students the total amount collected and remind them of the good things their contribution will help accomplish.

This service project helps children follow Jesus' call to love others and reminds them that we are all part of God's family.

Praying Together

Enabling children to pray with others is important during Lent and throughout the year. The following prayer can help the students express some of the meaning of the Lenten season in a way they can understand.

Divide the class into six small groups and assign one paragraph to each group. Print the prayer on the chalkboard or have each group memorize its paragraph. Begin the prayer with the sign of the cross. Then ask the first group to pray its part aloud. Continue in the same manner with the other groups.

God, Father and Creator,
we thank you for all the gifts
you have given us,
especially the gift of your Son.

During this holy season of Lent,
help us to change and grow
and become the kind of people
you created us to be.

Fill our hearts with love for you
and love for other people,
created in your image.

Show us how to use the gifts
you have given us
to help others in your name.

As we journey together
toward the light of Easter,
we know you are with us
in all that we do.

May we live always
as people of your kingdom
praising your name
now and forever.

Amen.

Conclude the prayer with the sign of the cross. This communal prayer is a way of calling on God's presence in during the Lenten season.

Forgiving Father Pantomime

The bible story of the forgiving Father is especially appropriate for Lent because it emphasizes God's love and mercy. In this echo pantomime story based on Luke 15:11-32 the children echo the words and actions of the leader as follows:

One day a son went to his father	*(walk in place)*
and said he was leaving home.	*(point in distance)*
He wanted money	*(hold palm up)*
so he could be on his own.	*(push away)*
The father gave him money	*(count money)*
and sent him on his way.	*(wave good-bye)*
The son spent all his money	*(pretend to throw)*
and soon had none.	*(hold palms up)*
He had to find a job	*(shade eyes)*
and soon was feeding pigs.	*(pretend to toss food)*
The son was very sad	*(finger points to mouth)*
and wanted to go home.	*(point in distance)*
He returned home to his father	*(walk in place)*
and said he was sorry.	*(fold hands)*
The father forgave the son	*(nod head)*
because he loved him.	*(hand on heart)*
God is like that father	*(nod head)*
because God always loves us.	*(hug self)*

This activity is guaranteed to hold the attention and interest of the children. An echo pantomime helps the children remember the Bible story and its meaning because they learn by doing.

Holy Card

A teacher-made holy card with a Bible verse and Christian symbol is an inexpensive yet heart-warming gift to give to the children at the beginning of Lent. A great time to present the holy card is right after the distribution of ashes on Ash Wednesday.

Select an appropriate scripture or liturgical verse for the holy card; for example, "Turn away from sin and be faithful to the gospel" from the Ash Wednesday liturgy. These words remind us that we are to move from selfishness toward the giving example of Jesus.

Print or type the verse in fancy script. Add an appropriate symbol such as a cross. Clip art books are a good source of Christian symbols. Print the parish name and date below the verse or on the other side of the card.

A good size to make a holy card is 2 3/4" x 5 1/2" (about one-sixth the size of a standard sheet of paper). Print six holy cards on one sheet of purple card stock paper and cut them apart.

The holy cards can be presented as part of a classroom or parish Ash Wednesday prayer service. These holy cards are a nice touch at the beginning of Lent. They can be used in many ways; as bookmarks, displayed on a home bulletin board, or carried in a shirt pocket.

Tissue Shamrock

St. Patrick is a beloved Irish saint, though he was born in England. We celebrate St. Patrick's feast day during Lent on March 17. According to legend, St. Patrick was kidnapped as a boy and taken to Ireland, but he later escaped. After returning to England he decided to become a priest.

Patrick then returned to Ireland as a missionary. He traveled all over Ireland teaching about God. He used the shamrock to explain to people the mystery of the Trinity, three persons in one God.

Children can remember the story of St. Patrick and his lesson about the Trinity by making tissue shamrocks.

Provide a shamrock pattern (approximately 9" high) and green construction paper. Each child also needs about fifty squares of green tissue paper, about 1 1/2" on a side. The tissue pieces do not need to be measured, however. The varying sizes look fine.

Tell the children to fold the tissue pieces around the eraser end of a pencil to form a three dimensional shape and then glue the tissue pieces to their shamrock.

Tape the finished shamrocks to a classroom wall before March 17. Have the children take home their shamrocks and a knowledge of St. Patrick and the Holy Trinity after St. Patrick's Day.

Cross Strip Calendar

Make a burlap calendar for the classroom to help count the weeks of Lent. Here's how to do it:

First, cut a strip of beige burlap, approximately 6" x 36". Fold the top inch of a width edge and sew a rod pocket. Fringe the bottom inch of the banner. Slip an 8" wooden dowel through the top and tie the ends with purple yarn to make a hanger. Hang the banner in the classroom.

Next, cut out six 4" x 5" crosses to represent the six weeks of Lent. The crosses can be of various styles: for example, the traditional Latin cross, St. Andrew's cross, and the Jerusalem. Consult a book of symbols for other shapes and styles of crosses. Use different colors of felt for each cross.

Glue one cross on the banner at the start of each new week of Lent. Use fabric glue for best results.

Each time a cross is added, draw the attention of the children to the calendar. Ask them which week of Lent the new cross represents and discuss ideas for living the Lenten season during the coming week.

Prayer Litany

St. Joseph is a model of faithfulness. We celebrate the feast of St. Joseph on March 19. Pray this litany in remembrance and appreciation of St. Joseph's example and for his ongoing intercession on our behalf:

St. Joseph, foster father of Jesus,
Pray for us.

St. Joseph, husband of Mary,
Pray for us.

St. Joseph, patron of the universal church,
Pray for us.

St. Joseph, model for workers,
Pray for us.

St. Joseph, patron of a happy death,
Pray for us.

St. Joseph, just and faithful person,
Pray for us.

This prayer reflects the many roles of St. Joseph and helps children appreciate his life of faith.

Haven Project

Family havens provide safe places for the victims of abuse and violence. Conduct a Lenten service project to benefit a family or women's shelter in your area.

Family havens have many day-to-day needs. Contact a local shelter through a referral agency to get a list of its most pressing needs. The addresses of shelters are often not advertised due to the need to protect the victims from further violence.

Give the list of needs to the children and their families. Ask them to take up a collection and bring the items to a place you have designated. Provide collection boxes.

A sample of typically needed items includes:

- cleaning products (dish soap, all-purpose cleaners)
- linens (towels, sheets)
- first aid supplies (aspirin, ice packs, cold medicine)
- household items (can opener, alarm clock)
- baby items (baby lotion, disposable diapers)
- paper products (bathroom tissue, paper towels)
- toiletries (toothbrushes, hairbrushes)
- craft items (glue, scissors, stickers)
- school supplies (pencils, notebook paper)

Many of the people who come to a haven do so in an emergency situation and are not able to bring even basic necessities with them. This service project fills a real need in the local community. It also helps students and their families reach out to others during Lent.

Reconciliation Prayer Service

A reconciliation prayer service is a way to remind the children that Lent is a season of mercy, forgiveness, and conversion.

Greeting

Leader: We gather to remember God's mercy and love. Our God is a kind and merciful God, always willing to forgive us.

Response: **All praise and glory to you, God.**

Opening Prayer

Reader: Merciful Father, we thank you for your love. Open our hearts and our minds to your presence. Help us to live as followers of your Son, Jesus Christ, and to ask forgiveness when we fail to do this. We ask this in your name.

Response: **Amen.**

Bible Reading

Reader: Let us listen to the story of the Forgiving Father. (Read Luke 15:11-32 from the Bible.) The word of the Lord.

Response: **Thanks be to God.**

Prayer of the Faithful

Leader: God calls us to love. Think about the times we have ignored this call. Let us ask for God's forgiveness.

Reader: For the times we have failed to pray and worship God,

Response: **Lord, have hear our prayer.**

Reader: For the times we have not treated other people fairly,

Response: **Lord, hear our prayer.**

Reader: For the times we have not helped those in need,

Response: **Lord, hear our prayer.**

Reader: For the times we have lied or cheated,

Response: **Lord, hear our prayer.**

Reader: For the times we have failed to forgive others,

Response: **Lord, hear our prayer.**

The Lord's Prayer

Leader: Let us pray the great prayer of reconciliation, the Our Father.
Our Father . . .

Sign of Peace

Reader: Lord, forgive us as we forgive others. As a sign of our reconciliation, we offer each other a sign of peace.

Response: **Peace be with you.**

Closing Prayer

Leader: Loving Father, we are your children. We thank you for the gift of your forgiveness and mercy. Help us to always follow Jesus Christ with the help of the Holy Spirit.

Response: **Amen.**

If you will have individual confessions, ask the students to proceed to the area you have reserved.

Palm Parade

On Passion, or Palm Sunday we enter the holiest week of the year. The feast marks Jesus' final entrance into Jerusalem prior to his death.

A wonderful addition to a lesson about Passion Sunday is a palm parade with several grade-levels of children participating. Have the students assemble out of doors with their teachers. Provide palm branches. Ask some of the older students to distribute the palms to younger children. Also, encourage the older students to make and carry posters that proclaim "Hosanna" or "Jesus is Lord".

For the parade, dress one person in a red cloak and provide him or her with a wood cross. Have the other students follow this leader around the church property while waving their palms.

The procession should lead to the church, gym, or other pre-selected meeting space for a prayer service. The prayer service should include a blessing of the palms and a reading describing Jesus' triumphant entry into Jerusalem (for example, Matthew 21:1-11). Finally, have the children sing a familiar Holy Week song.

This activity and prayer experience helps the children gain a greater feel for what it was like on the first Palm Sunday.

Choral Reading

The following choral reading can be used on or near Passion Sunday to help the children celebrate Christ's coming as king. Assign readers and allow them to practice their parts prior to the reading.

Reader 1:	When Jesus rode a donkey small
	All the people began to call:
All:	**Hosanna to the King!**
Reader 2:	Coats and flowers before him lay
	Then all the crowds could be heard to say:
All:	**Hosanna to the King!**
Reader 3:	Palm branches they waved as he rode along
	Their songs of praise were growing loud and strong!
All:	**Hosanna to the King!**
Reader 4:	Little children made the hillsides ring
	And Jesus smiled to hear them sing:
All:	**Hosanna to the King!**
Reader 5:	Into Jerusalem Jesus came
	Men, women, and children were calling his name:
All:	**Hosanna to the King!**
Reader 6:	Since Jesus came to die for me
	My song to him shall always be:
All:	**Hosanna to the King!**

This reading can also be used with preschool children. In that situation, the teacher can read all the parts and have the children chime in with the refrain.

Passion Banner

Provide each child with a piece of 8 1/2″ x 11″ red construction paper to use as a passion banner. Red is the liturgical color for Passion Sunday. Have the children follow these steps to make individual paper banners to remind them of the lesson of Passion Sunday:

First, cut a 7″ cross from white construction paper and glue it to the middle of banner. If possible, add a gold cross sticker to the center of the cross. Next, cut a palm (about 7″ long) from green construction paper. Glue the palm to the banner at an angle at the foot of the cross.

This mini-banner can be posted at home. The palm and the cross are reminders of the Passion Sunday gospel and the events of Holy Week.

Triduum Prayer

The following prayer service is part of a lesson on the Triduum. The teacher reads the part of the leader and three pre-selected children each read one of the petitions. The entire class joins in the response.

Leader: Dear Jesus, we gather together today to recall the events of the Triduum. This is a holy time when we celebrate your saving death and triumphant resurrection.

Child 1: You gave us the gift of the eucharist on Holy Thursday. May we always live as your people.

All: **You are our light and our hope.**

Child 2: You died on a cross on Good Friday. Help us to die to all things that keep us from following you.

All: **You are our light and our hope.**

Child 3: You rose to new life on Easter. May we always live as your creation and proclaim the good news to all people.

All: **You are our light and our hope.**

Leader: We thank you for all you have done for us. We pray that all people will come to see your life, death, and resurrection as a sign of hope. We ask this in your name.

All: **Amen.**

Praying this prayer together helps students to recall the events of the paschal mystery and to celebrate the victory of Christ's resurrection.

Agape Service

An agape service is a shared meal of love. Prepare a table in the classroom or meeting area with a tablecloth and a candle. Place an unsliced loaf of bread on the table with a pitcher of grape juice. You will also need a napkin and small paper cup for each child.

Tell the children they will celebrate a meal in remembrance of the meals Jesus shared with his friends, especially his final meal with them on Holy Thursday. Then begin the following agape service.

Opening Greeting

Leader: Jesus shared many meals with his friends. Today, we recall his final meal, his Last Supper on Holy Thursday.

Litany

Leader: Lord, Jesus, you love and forgive us no matter what we do.

All: **For this we thank you, Jesus.**

Leader: Lord, Jesus because of your example we forgive those who hurt us.

All: **For this we thank you, Jesus.**

Leader: Lord Jesus, you suffered and died for us.

All: **For this we thank you, Jesus.**

Leader: Lord Jesus, you rose from the dead and opened the gates of heaven.

All: **For this we thank you, Jesus.**

Prayer of Forgiveness

Leader: Now let us take a moment of silence to tell Jesus we are sorry for anything we have done wrong. (Pause.) We also ask each other's forgiveness through an exchange of peace. (The children share the gesture of peace.) May God bless us as we remember his Son, our Lord Jesus Christ. (Make the sign of the cross.)

All: **Amen.**

Sharing of Meal

Leader: We will now share the bread and grape juice as a remembrance of the food shared at the Last Supper. (Let each child break off a piece of bread from the loaf and eat it. Also give each child a small cup of grape juice to drink.)

Closing Prayer

Leader: Let us pray. God, we thank you for your goodness. Continue to bless us, Lord, all the days of our life. We will forever thank you and sing your praise.

All: **It is right to give God thanks and praise. Amen.**

Prayer Card

Have the children make a Holy Thursday prayer card for their family dinner table. The following prayer can be used:

~Prayer for Holy Thursday~

Jesus, at the Last Supper
you gave the gift of yourself in
the bread and wine.

May we come together often
to celebrate your gift of eucharist.

Help us to share our lives
with others as you share yourself
with us. Amen.

Duplicate a copy of the prayer for each student on half sheets of white paper. Also give each child a full sheet of purple construction paper. Have them fold the purple paper in half widthwise. Make sure they press the crease firmly so that the prayer card will stand up. Finally, have them use a glue stick to attach the prayer below the fold of the construction paper.

The prayer can be read by one person or shared as mealtime grace. This prayer encourages the children to share with their families what they are learning about Holy Thursday and the Triduum.

Last Supper Pantomime

The events of the Last Supper can be shared with children during a lesson on Holy Thursday. In an echo pantomime, after the teacher says a line and does the appropriate motions, the children echo what they have seen and heard.

While they were eating,	*(eating motions)*
Jesus took the bread.	*(pull in arm toward body)*
He blessed it,	*(fold hands in prayer)*
broke it,	*(pull hands apart)*
and gave it to his disciples.	*(hands together, palms up)*
Jesus said,	*(hand by mouth)*
Take this and eat:	*(eating motions)*
THIS IS MY BODY.	*(arms outstretched)*
Do this in memory of me.	*(hands on heart, head bowed)*
Then he took the cup.	*(pull in arm toward body)*
He gave thanks	*(fold hands in prayer)*
and gave it to his disciples.	*(hands together, palms up)*
Jesus said,	*(hand by mouth)*
Take this and drink:	*(drinking motion)*
THIS IS MY BLOOD.	*(arms outstretched)*
Do this in memory of me.	*(hands on heart, head bowed)*
This was Jesus' Last Supper.	*(eating motions)*
Then he went out	*(walk in place)*
to his death	*(head bowed)*
and his resurrection.	*(arms raised over head)*

This echo pantomime helps the children become familiar with the events of Holy Thursday that are recreated at each Mass.

Mass Ideas

The days surrounding Holy Thursday are good times to help the children learn about the parts of the Mass and the important role of the assembly. Listed below are brief explanations of the Mass parts and suggestions for sharing this information with children.

~Gathering Rite~

Entrance: We gather together as a community.

—Learn one of the processional songs sung at Mass.

Greeting: We are welcomed in the name of Jesus Christ.

—Talk about the church as a community of God's people.

Sign of the Cross: This is a reminder of our belief in the Trinity.

—Explain to the children that making the sign of the cross means that we believe in God—Father, Son, and Holy Spirit.

Gloria: We praise and thank God.

—Have the children work together to decorate a "Glory to God" mural for the classroom.

~Liturgy of the Word~

First Reading: We listen to a reading from the Bible.

—As an example of a first reading, read Acts 2:42-47. Ask the children what these words tell us about the early church.

Psalm Response: The psalms are songs of praise.

—Share a beautiful psalm of thanksgiving, for example Psalm 136.

Second Reading: We listen to a reading from the Bible.

—As an example of a second reading, read John 4:7-10.

Gospel: We listen carefully to a story about Jesus.

—Have the children act or pantomime one of the gospel stories, for example the story of the Good Samaritan (Luke 10:29-42).

Homily: We learn to live the Word of God in our lives.

—Discuss how each of us is called to be a follower of Jesus Christ.

Profession of Faith: The creed is a summary of our beliefs.

—Ask the children to name some of the things that we believe as Christians.

Prayers of the Faithful: We pray for our needs and the needs of others.

—Compose prayer litany with the class and pray for those in need.

~Liturgy of the Eucharist~

Presentation of Gifts: We offer bread, wine, and ourselves to God.

—Have the students create a posterboard collage of God's many gifts using magazine photographs.

Eucharistic Prayer: We thank God, especially for the gift of God's Son, Jesus Christ.

—Have the students memorize one or more Memorial Acclamation.

~Communion Rite~

Our Father: We pray together the prayer that Jesus taught us.

—Pray the Our Father with gestures.

Sign of Peace: We are to be peacemakers in our world.

—Share the peace prayer of St. Francis. Give each child a copy of the prayer to take home.

Communion: Jesus shares his very life with us.

—Read a gospel story of the Last Supper (for example, Mark 14:22-26) to the class.

~Dismissal Rite~

Blessing: We ask God's blessing on all we do.

—Have the children draw and color a cross as a sign of the Trinity.

Dismissal: We go forth to live what we believe.

—Participate in a service project such as collecting cans of food for a food pantry.

Remembering with Rocks

Using rocks and a guided meditation, children can experience the events of the Triduum in a unique way. Purchase small white rocks from a garden store and put them in a basket in the front of the room. Invite each child to come forward one at a time and choose a rock to hold. Then read the following meditation.

Did you know that Jesus was probably born in a cave? The land around Bethlehem was hilly and rocky and had many caves. A cave is really an opening in a big rock ledge. Look at your rock. Feel it. Imagine that it could have once been part of a cave.

Much later in his life, the night before he died, in fact, Jesus went to a garden to pray. Peter, James, and John were with him for company, but they kept falling asleep. Jesus was alone and afraid. The Bible says he even cried. The only thing holding up Jesus' body was a rock. He knelt down by the rock. He rested his arms on the rock. He laid his head on the rock and used it like a pillow. The rock was washed clean by Jesus' tears.

Then the soldiers came to the garden to arrest Jesus. A trial was held for Jesus and he was unjustly sentenced to death on a cross. Barefoot, Jesus was forced to carry the wood for the cross over stony streets.

Look again at your rock. Is it hard? Is it sharp? If you fell on a pile of rocks like the one you're holding, would your knees get scraped and cut? The path Jesus walked with the cross was rocky and he fell under his cross three times.

When Jesus came to the hill where he was to die, the soldiers used a big rock to pound the nails that held Jesus to the cross. They probably also piled rocks at the based of the cross to hold it in place.

Jesus was buried in a cave. A huge rock was rolled in front of the opening. Jesus' friends and mother never before felt so miserable. This mood disappeared completely on Easter Sunday. The cave was opened. The large rock was rolled back. Jesus is risen!

Look at your rock. Take it home and put it in a special place where you can see it and remember Jesus and the events of Holy Thursday, Good Friday, and Easter Sunday. Tell others about your rock and why it is so special.

Calvary Prayer

Calvary is the name of the hill outside of Jerusalem where Jesus was crucified. The following prayer can help the children think about the importance and meaning that Jesus' death on a cross holds for them. Ask the children to quiet themselves, close their eyes, and rest their heads on a table, if possible. Then read these words slowly and meditatively.

Father, we walk with Jesus
as he carries his cross to Calvary.
Help us to pick ourselves up again when we fall
as Jesus did when he collapsed
under the weight of the cross.

We pause today to remember all those things
that we have said and done
which have hurt you
and have hurt other people.

Forgive us, Father,
for the wrong we have done.

We are sorry for the times
we have not been fair,
we have not helped others,
we have lied,
we have said mean things.

Help us to make good choices
and to be caring people.

Through his suffering, death, and resurrection
Jesus brings us new life and new hope.

Father, help us to share this good news
with others.
We ask you this through your Son,
Jesus Christ, our Lord.

Amen.

Twig Cross

A twig cross is a traditional craft project to mark Good Friday.

For this craft each child needs two twigs. If possible, take the class outside as a group and have them find their own twigs. Show them the types of twigs that will work best: one thick twig at least 10″ long, and a thinner twig at least 7″ long.

Back in the classroom, have the students lay the shorter twig across the longer piece as a crossbar. Provide green yarn. Demonstrate how to wrap the yarn around the twigs where they intersect.

Remind the children that Good Friday is about life, not only death. To emphasize this give each child a small spray of white silk flowers. Bunches of silk flowers can be purchased inexpensively at craft stores and cut apart for this project. One bunch will decorate several crosses. Have the children attach the flowers to the center of the cross by wrapping the yarn around them in the same manner as before. Help the children securely tie the two ends. Cut the excess yarn close to the cross.

These wooden crosses help the children remember the events of Good Friday and the promise of Easter. They can be taken home and displayed during Holy Week and afterwards as a reminder of God's love.

Good Friday Story

Using six plastic Easter eggs and six symbols of Jesus' passion, you can present the story of Good Friday in a way that children are not likely to forget. To begin, number six plastic eggs, 1 to 6, with self-adhesive labels. Before class, place the following items in each egg:

Egg 1: a small twig of thorns from a rosebush
Egg 2: two small wooden sticks
Egg 3: a small piece of sponge with vinegar
Egg 4: a piece of white fabric
Egg 5: a stone
Egg 6: whole cloves

Begin the presentation by briefly reviewing the events that led to the arrest of Jesus. Then read aloud the text from Matthew 27:29:

> Weaving a crown out of thorns, they placed it on his head, and a reed in his right hand. And kneeling before him, they mocked him, saying, Hail, King of the Jews.

Open up Egg 1 and show its contents. Pass the egg around the room. Ask the children to pray silently, imagining the pain and humiliation that Jesus experienced.

Collect Egg 1 and read the following verse from Matthew 27:32:

> As they were going out, they met a Cyrenian named Simon; this man they pressed into service to carry his cross.

Open Egg 2 and show its contents. Pass the egg around the room. Ask the children to pray for the courage to help Jesus carry his cross.

Collect Egg 2 and read the verse from Matthew 27:48:

> Immediately one of them ran to get a sponge: he soaked it in wine and putting it on a reed, gave it to him to drink.

Open Egg 3 and show its contents. Pass it around the room and ask the children to smell it and imagine Jesus' thirst and the humiliation he felt when he was given the vinegar.

Collect Egg 3 and read the following passage from Matthew 27:59:

Taking the body, Joseph wrapped it in clean linen.

Display the contents of Egg 4. Point out that this cloth reminds us of the burial cloth of Jesus. Pass the Egg around and ask the students to reflect on the despair Jesus' friends must have felt when he died.

Collect Egg 4 and read the verse from Matthew 27:60:

> And laid it in his new tomb that he had hewn in the rock. Then he rolled a huge stone across the entrance to the tomb and departed.

Explain to the children that people were sometimes buried in caves. Show the contents of Egg 5 and pass it around. Ask the children to pray for someone they know who has died.

Collect egg 5. Read this final verse from Mark 16:1:

> When the Sabbath was over, Mary Magdalene, Mary, the mother of James, and Salome bought spices so they might go and anoint him.

Open Egg 6 and show the cloves. As Egg 6 is passed around, add to the story of Jesus' resurrection and appearances to his friends. Explain that though Jesus was gone from the tomb, he had risen from the dead so that we might all have new life.

This activity engages and holds the attention of the students. It is an interesting way of helping students learn about the passion of Jesus and the events surrounding Good Friday.

Chapter 4

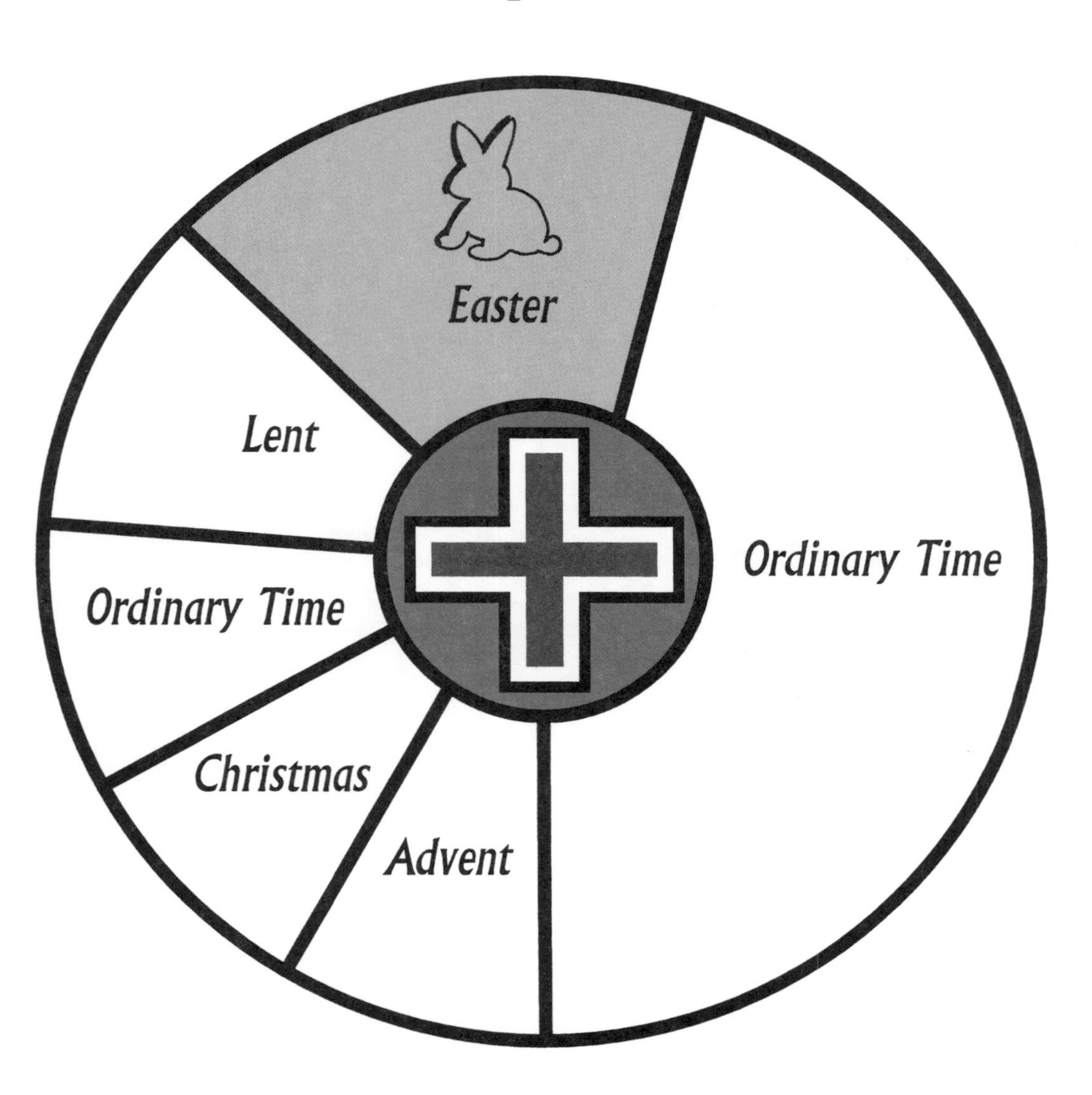

~Easter~

We Rejoice in the Risen Lord

Thomas answered and said to him,
"My Lord and my God."
~John 20:28~

Easter is at the heart of our Christian faith. Without a strong, unswerving belief in the resurrection of Christ, then, as St. Paul writes, "empty too is our preaching; empty too your faith" (1 Corinthians 15:14).

The Easter season lasts for fifty days, from Easter Sunday until Pentecost Sunday. The liturgical colors are white, the Gloria and gospel alleluia are returned to the liturgy, and all signs point to the joy of the season.

Jesus' resurrection was first evidenced not only by the empty tomb but by his many appearances to his disciples. These experiences of the risen Christ in the lives of the disciples and the coming of the Holy Spirit, transformed a group of frightened followers into dynamic witnesses who first spread the message of good news.

At liturgy, the lit paschal candle reminds us that Jesus is with us. We experience the risen Christ in many ways: in our daily actions, through family and friends, in the proclaimed Word, in the blessed gifts of bread and wine. With Thomas we profess, "My Lord and my God."

As people of the resurrection we bring the good news of Easter to others. We share the great joy that accompanies the promised gift of everlasting life. And, as did the first disciples, we don't do this alone: Jesus sent the Holy Spirit to guide our lives and our church. Alive in the Spirit, we go forth to give glory to God's name by all we say and do.

This chapter offers projects, activities, and prayers to help children live more fully the wonderment of Easter and Pentecost.

Felt Banner

The butterfly is a traditional and wonderful symbol of the resurrection. Children can learn about this symbol by creating a colorful butterfly mini-banner from felt.

Provide each child with a 6″x 9″ piece of blue felt. Have the children make a one-inch fold at the top of one width edge and glue it in place to make a rod pocket. As a decorative touch, have them notch the opposite edge of the banner with scissors.

Next, have each child cut out two 3″ wide felt butterflies. Provide patterns if necessary. The choice of various bright colors should be left to each individual child. Tell the children to position and glue their butterflies onto the banner with craft glue.

After the glue has dried, have the children place a wooden dowel (approximately 7″ long) through the rod pocket. Provide a 9″ length of yarn to tie to both ends of the dowel to make a hanger.

These completed banners proclaim the hope of new life. Without words, they speak of the wonder and glory of Easter so that even young children can understand.

Diamante Poem

Children enjoy writing poetry, especially when they have a simple form to follow. The diamante poem has seven lines and, when printed, is shaped like a diamond. Use this form to encourage the children to express their feelings about Easter.

Write the following instructions on posterboard or the chalkboard so all can see:

- Write "Easter" on the first line.
- On the second line, write two words to describe the season.
- On the third line, write three words that are symbolic of the season.
- On the fourth line, write a four-word phrase expressing a Christian belief about Jesus.
- On the fifth line, write three other words symbolic of the Easter season.
- On the sixth line, write two words that can be addressed to Jesus in prayer.
- On the last line, write a one-word summary; for example, "Alleluia."

Work through a class diamante on the board to help the students get the hang of the concept. Then allow time for the students to compose their own individual Easter diamante poems. A sample diamante follows:

Easter
new life
cross tomb prayer
Jesus Christ is risen today
lilies butterflies dawn
God's love
Alleluia

Encourage the students to share their poems with others as a witness of their belief in the Easter event.

New Life Wreath

A new life wreath is an Easter version of the traditional Christmas wreath. Actually the circular shape is a perfect sign of Easter, representing the eternal life guaranteed by the resurrection.

Have each child cut out a wreath—about 9″ in diameter—from a sheet of green construction paper. Distribute two strips of pink ribbon for them to glue to the bottom of the wreath. New life symbols can be included on the wreath to give it an Easter touch; for example, a sun, flower, egg, bunny, or butterfly. The symbols can be drawn by the children or you can provide stickers depicting these and other new life items.

The new life wreath can be displayed on a door, wall, or mirror. Children are delighted with this wreath and it is a great reminder of Easter that can last the duration of the Easter season.

Resurrection Prayer Service

We can express the hope of Easter with the children through a classroom prayer service.

Choose readers to take the various parts. The teacher can take the role of leader. All the students participate by listening to the readings, sharing responses, and singing the songs.

Opening Song

Rejoice! He Lives! (Young People's Glory and Praise II).

Opening Prayer

Leader: God, we thank you for sending Jesus to bring us new life through his life, death, and resurrection. We gather together to celebrate Easter and to praise you for your glory.

All: **May we always live as your people.**

Lighting of the Easter Candle

Leader: Today we light the Easter candle as a sign that the risen Christ is with us. (Light large candle.)

All: **Glory and Praise to our God.**

Bible Reading

Reader: A reading from the gospel of Luke (24:1-6,9):

But at daybreak on the first day of the week they took spices they had prepared and went to the tomb. They found the stone rolled away from the tomb: but when they entered, they did not find the body of the Lord Jesus. While they were puzzling over this, behold, two men in dazzling garments appeared to them. They were terrified and bowed their faces to the ground. They said to them, "Why do you seek the living one among the dead? He is not here, but has been raised." Then they returned from the tomb and announced all these things to the eleven and to all the others. The word of the Lord.

All: **Thanks be to God.**

Offering

Leader: We now offer our prayers of thanksgiving for all God has done for us. (Children come forward one at a time and place individual prayers written on butterfly patterns in front of the altar, or pray aloud for personal needs.)

Prayer Response

Leader: We pray together as a community of God's people.

Reader: On Easter Jesus rose from the dead.

All: **Jesus is risen. Alleluia.**

Reader: He appeared to his disciples.

All: **Jesus is risen. Alleluia.**

Reader: He makes us a new creation.

All: **Jesus is risen. Alleluia.**

Reader: He calls us to follow him.

All **Jesus is risen. Alleluia.**

Reader: He has come for all people.

All: **Jesus is risen. Alleluia.**

Closing Prayer

Leader: Father, help us to be committed to the risen Christ. May your kingdom shine through our lives and actions. May we walk always in the light of your love. We pray this in the name of your Son, Jesus Christ.

All: **Amen. Alleluia.**

Closing Song

Easter People (Young People's Glory and Praise II).

Sticker Poem

Decorating an Easter poem with new life stickers can help children understand more of the meaning of this great feast.

Print following poem in calligraphy or type it in fancy script:

~Easter Poem~

Jesus has risen
from the dead
on Easter Sunday
as he said.

Because of Jesus
we shout and say
alleluia, alleluia,
happy Easter day.

Make copies in various spring colors and give one copy to each student.

Have the children decorate the poem with Easter stickers such as the risen Christ, lilies, butterflies, and flowers. Show them how to place a sticker at the end of the first line, the beginning of the third, end of the fifth, and beginning of the seventh line. A slightly larger sheet of darker, but brightly-colored construction paper can back the poem to form a frame.

Intention Tree

A terrific way to encourage petitional prayer during the Easter season is the "intention tree." The children write their personal intentions on butterfly cut outs and hang them on a tree." A branch brought in from outside and placed in a pot or a small decorative white tree purchased from a craft store work well for this project.

Trace butterfly symbols on different colors of construction paper and duplicate enough so that children have plenty of choice of colors.

Explain what you mean by intentions. Intentions are whatever needs, large or small, a child wants to pray for. For example, a child may write a prayer for a sick pet, a dying relative, world peace, good grades, suffering due to war, homeless people, or family problems.

After the children have written their intentions and signed their initials on the butterfly, have them cut the butterfly out, punch a hole through the top, and feed and tie a piece of yarn through the hole. Each butterfly is then hung on a branch.

Choose one intention to pray especially for each day the children are in class. The intention tree reminds the children to pray for their own needs and the needs of others.

This idea can also be used during other seasons by changing the symbols. Leaves can be used in the fall, snowflakes during the winter, crosses during Lent, and flowers in the summer.

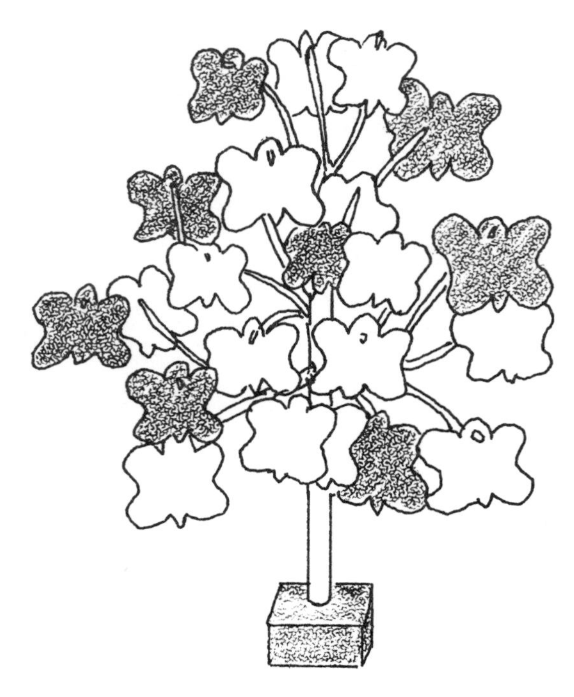

Easter Acrostic

In an acrostic, a word is formed from the first letters of a phrase. Use the word "Easter" as the starting point for a prayer of praise and thanksgiving.

Have each student vertically print the word Easter in upper case letters down the left side of a sheet of paper. Next, ask them to write six phrases about the Easter season using each letter as the starting point. For example:

E njoy God's creation
A ll the nations praise our God
S end the Holy Spirit to us
Tell the good news
E very person has new life
R ejoice in the Lord always

The activity can be enhanced through the use of colorful markers. Don't use yellow, however. It is too light to be read. Finally, ask the students to illustrate the borders of their Easter acrostic with appropriate Easter symbols in the margins of the paper.

Writing an Easter acrostic not only gives students an outlet for their thoughts and ideas, but helps them stop and reflect on the joy and hope of the Easter season.

Planting Flowers

Blooming flowers are a beautiful sign of the new life initiated at Easter. Children can share this joy of new life by planting flowers. If possible, arrange for the children to plant flowers on church grounds. Check with the person in charge of landscaping before beginning the project. Another option is to plant flowers at the home of an elderly parishioner.

It is easiest for children to plant small flowers that have already grown from seed. Pick a hardy flower such as marigolds or begonias. These bedding plants produce a quick infusion of color in a bare area. Check with a local nursery to see if these plants can be donated to you for this project.

Have the children dig holes in the dirt using a garden trowel or large spoon. The hole must be deep enough to cover the roots of the flower. Then, have the children carefully remove the individual flower from its container, place it in the hole, and fill the space around the plant with dirt to keep it in place.

Arrange for watering and maintenance needs. If possible, schedule future class times for the children to water and care for the flowers as well as to witness their growth.

Alleluia Song

Young children can express their enthusiasm for Easter through a simple song. The following words are sung to the tune of "Mary Had A Little Lamb."

~Jesus Is Risen~

Jesus Christ is risen today,
risen today, risen today.
Jesus Christ is risen today,
Alleluia.

He has come for one and all,
one and all, one and all.
He has come for one and all,
Alleluia.

Jesus brings new life to us,
life to us, life to us,
Jesus brings new life to us.
Alleluia.

This is an easy song for the children to learn. In singing these lyrics the children indeed make a joyful noise unto the Lord!

Egg Tree

An outdoor egg tree is a simple group project that involves all the children in the class. Scout out a nearby tree with branches low enough for the children to reach. The only other supplies needed are colorful plastic Easter eggs (one or two per student), string, and scissors.

Cut six inch lengths of string. Show the children how to put both ends of the string into the top half of the egg and then close the bottom half over it. The string is secured inside the egg and a loop is formed outside the egg for hanging. Help any children who are having difficulty.

Let the students choose where they want to hang their eggs on the tree. Each egg should be hung a few inches back on a branch, preferably behind a twig. This will secure it from falling off in the breeze.

The tree is a reminder to all that Easter lasts for more than one day and that we are always continually striving to be resurrection people.

Colorful Butterfly

Young children can make colorful paper butterflies as a reminder that Easter is a time of new beginnings and new hope because of Jesus Christ. The butterfly is a traditional resurrection symbol since it comes forth from a cocoon in a way reminiscent of Jesus' rising from the tomb on Easter Sunday.

Provide each child with a half sheet of construction paper. Offer a variety of colors. Also provide an 8" butterfly pattern as a cutting guide.

When the butterflies have been cut out, have the children decorate them with stickers that represent the new life of spring. Stickers of flowers, birds, sun, butterflies, and trees are readily available. Five stickers are needed for each butterfly.

Demonstrate how to fold the wings of the butterfly by creasing it in the middle. Display the butterflies in the classroom throughout the Easter season. The children will be pleased with how the butterflies brightly decorate their environment.

Thomas Pantomime

This echo pantomime tells the story of "doubting" Thomas. It is based on John 20:19-29, a gospel we hear proclaimed during the Easter season. The students echo the teacher's words and actions line by line.

After his resurrection	*(swing arms upward)*
Jesus came to his disciples,	*(arms outstretched)*
"Peace be with you,"	*(clasp hands together)*
he said to them.	*(hands cup mouth)*
The apostles rejoiced	*(extend arms over head)*
when they saw him alive.	*(nod head)*
Jesus said to them,	*(hands cup mouth)*
"As the Father has sent me,	*(point to chest)*
so I send you	*(point to others)*
to teach all people."	*(swing arm in arc)*
Thomas was not there	*(shake head no)*
when Jesus came to them.	*(arms outstretched)*
The disciples said,	*(hands cup mouth)*
"We have seen the Lord."	*(nod head)*
Thomas said to them,	*(hands cup mouth)*
"Unless I see his nail marks,	*(touch palms with finger)*
I will not believe."	*(shake head no)*
A week later Jesus came	*(arms outstretched)*
and said to Thomas,	*(hands cup mouth)*
"See my hands."	*(touch palms with finger)*
Thomas said to him,	*(hands cup mouth)*
"My Lord and my God"	*(bow head and fold hands)*
Jesus told him,	*(hands cup mouth)*
"Blessed are those	*(nod head)*
who have not seen,	*(point to eyes)*
but who believe in me."	*(arms outstretched)*

Follow this echo pantomime with a discussion about the meaning of faith. Ask the children what evidence they have witnessed that Jesus is God.

Symbol Prayer

Using springtime symbols in a classroom prayer service helps make the prayer more meaningful for young children.

Have each child draw one of the following Easter or springtime symbols: a candle, butterfly, egg, sun, flowers, or lamb on a piece of 8 1/2" x 11" posterboard. As you or an adult leader reads the following prayer service, invite the children with the specific symbols to hold them over their heads when you read their part.

Candle (hold up symbol):

Christ lights up our world. There is new life at Easter.

All: **Alleluia. Alleluia. Alleluia.**

Butterfly (hold up symbol):

The cocoon, caterpillar, and beautiful butterfly help us learn about dying and rising. There is new life at Easter.

All: **Alleluia. Alleluia. Alleluia.**

Egg (hold up symbol):

The shell breaks open. A chick appears. There is new life at Easter.

All: **Alleluia. Alleluia. Alleluia.**

Sun (hold up symbol):

The sun shines brightly on Easter day. Jesus is risen! There is new life at Easter.

All: **Alleluia. Alleluia. Alleluia.**

Flowers (hold up symbol):

The little seed looked dead, until it broke through the earth and blossomed for all to see. There is new life at Easter.

All: **Alleluia. Alleluia. Alleluia.**

Lamb (hold up symbol):

The lamb wobbles to its feet as it discovers the joy of springtime air. There is new life at Easter.

All: **Alleluia. Alleluia. Alleluia.**

This prayer helps children celebrate the Easter season. It enables them to pray to God in a way they can understand.

Helping the Hungry

Food for the Poor (550 S.W. 12th Avenue, Deerfield Beach, FL 33442) is an organization which helps poor people in Caribbean nations with food and other supplies. This group works with missionaries, religious orders, and church groups who serve in these poor areas. It provides for a variety of needs to hospitals, children's homes, and other charities. Items purchased with monetary donations to Food for the Poor include food, lumber, clothes, beds, sewing machines, and medical and educational supplies.

Encourage the children to contribute money during the Easter season to an agency which helps to feed the hungry, like Food for the Poor. Send information to the parents about the particular organization that will receive your group's donations. Decorate a coffee can and put a slit in the plastic lid to make a container to put donations. Print the name of the organization on the outside of the can. Provide similar collection cans in other locations.

This activity provides a good extension to similar projects undertaken during Lent. It reminds the children that we are called to see Jesus in the faces of the poor during the Easter season and throughout the year.

Mosaic Egg

Spring is filled with signs of new life. When we see new buds on trees, flowers blooming, and baby birds in their nest, we are reminded of the ever-repeating cycle of life. In a similar way, the egg is a popular symbol of the Easter season.

Mosaic eggs are a simple craft for children to make and a way to reinforce this lesson. This project requires colorful construction paper, glue, and a child's creativity. Have the children cut out large paper eggs from half sheets of construction paper. A variety of colors makes the project more fun.

Tell the children they are to tear small pieces of construction paper that can fit on their eggs. The pieces do not have to be exactly the same size. Then, have them glue the torn pieces in colorful rows. Preferably, each row should be all one color and the pieces should overlap one another. When complete, the entire surface of the egg should be covered with colorful rows of torn paper. The final step is to trim any extra paper off the edges of the egg for a smooth oval shape.

The feature of this project is that each egg turns out differently. These colorful eggs make a wonderful classroom display.

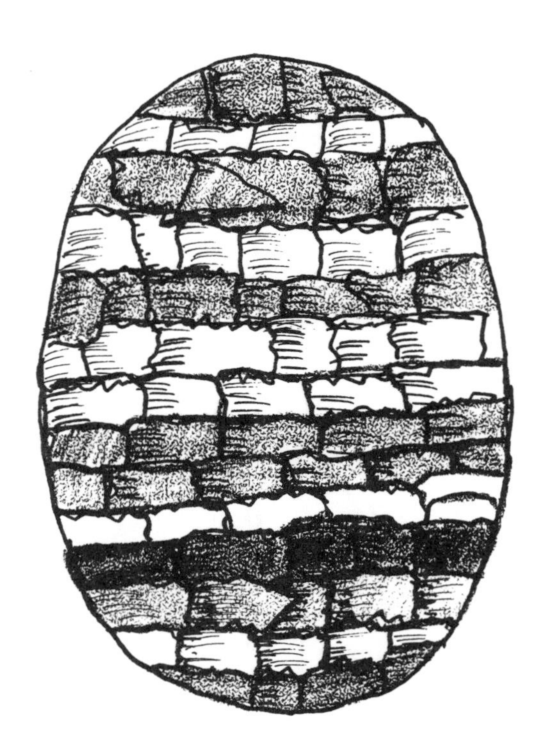

Butterfly Prayer

Children should be encouraged to pray to God in their own words. One interesting way to teach spontaneous prayer at Easter time is with the following butterfly prayer activity.

Draw an outline of a butterfly widthwise to cover an entire unlined standard size sheet of paper. Inside the butterfly draw horizontal lines using a pen and ruler. On the top line print the words "My Easter Prayer." You now have a sheet of butterfly stationery! Duplicate one sheet for each student in the class.

Ask the students to write short, individual, Easter-theme prayers on their butterfly stationery. Also, tell the children to sign their names. A butterfly prayer turns out like this:

When the students are finished, call on volunteers to share their prayers with the class.

The butterfly prayers can be used as an offering at a prayer service or taken home to be shared with parents.

Meditation

The following is a prayer meditation to be used during the Easter season. It helps us to recall the meaning of Jesus' resurrection. Ask for five student volunteers to read the parts of the prayer. All of the rest of the children offer the response.

Reader 1: Jesus, on the first Easter Sunday
the angel told Mary Magdalene
that you had risen from the dead.

All: **May we proclaim**
the good news of your resurrection to others.
Hear us, risen Lord.

Reader 2: Jesus, the travelers on the road to Emmaus
recognized you
in the breaking of the bread.

All: **May we also know you**
through celebrating the eucharist together.
Hear us, risen Lord.

Reader 3: Jesus, you appeared to your apostles
and said to them,
"Peace be with you."

All: **May we be a people**
of justice and peace in our world.
Hear us, risen Lord.

Reader 4: Jesus, forty days after Easter
you ascended to the right hand of the Father.

All: **May we always remember God's great love**
and share it with others.
Hear us, risen Lord.

Reader 5: Jesus, on Pentecost you sent the Holy Spirit
to guide your followers.

All: **May we follow the Spirit in our lives,**
now and always.
Hear us, risen Lord.

Baby Layettes

A layette is a basic collection of clothing and baby items like diapers and lotion that are needed to care for a new baby. Many charitable organizations provide layettes for mothers and families in need.

Begin a service project during the Easter season to collect items to donate for baby layettes. Explain the project to the children and send a note to the parents enlisting family support. Also, publicize the project in the parish bulletin. Include a list of requested items and the name of the organization that will be distributing the layettes. Items on this list might include the following:

gown — *diapers*
shirt — *outfit*
bibs — *pacifier*
blanket — *sweater*

Be sure to check with the organization that provides the layettes as to exactly what baby items are most needed.

Provide clearly-marked collection boxes at a central location at the school or parish. See that all items are promptly forwarded to the distributing organization. Be sure to thank all participants and let them know how many complete layettes were made possible through their contributions.

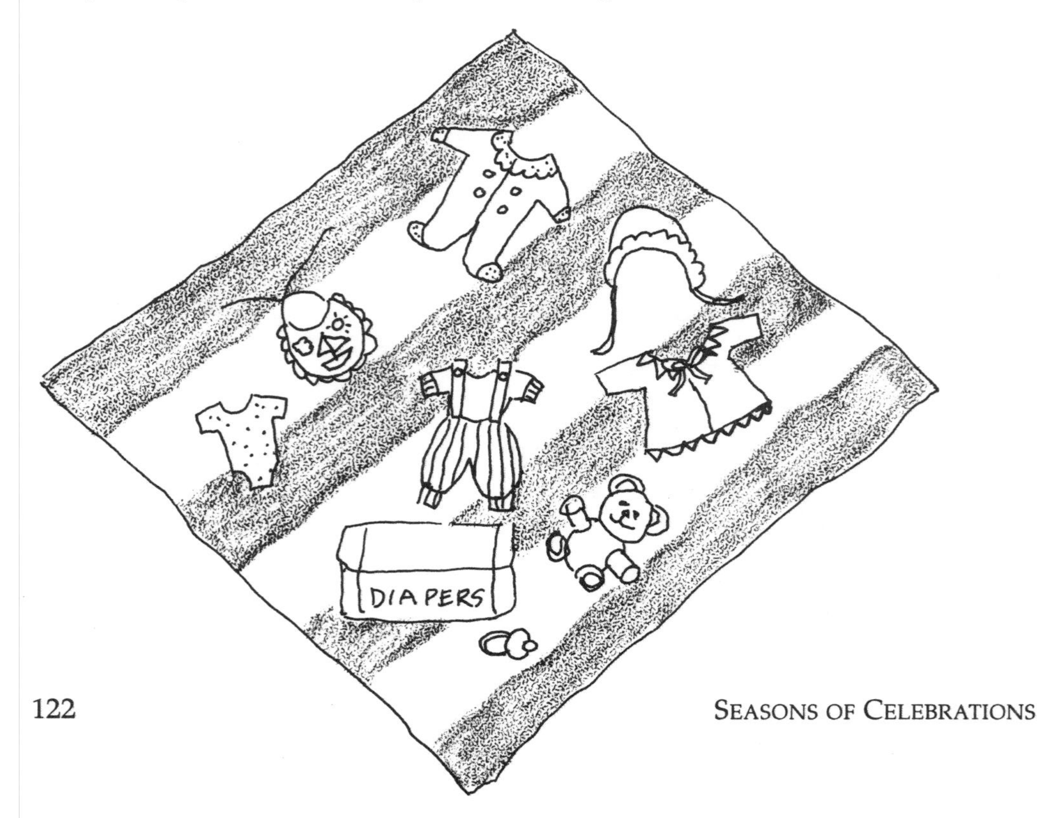

Catch of Fish Pantomime

The following echo pantomime is based on Jesus' appearance to the disciples at the sea of Tiberius (John 21:1-12). The children echo the words and actions of the teacher for each line.

Peter and six others	*(count on fingers)*
were on the lake in a boat.	*(rowing motions)*
They fished all night	*(hands together beside head)*
but did not catch any fish.	*(shake head no)*
When the sun came up	*(stretch arms and yawn)*
they saw a man on shore.	*(hand shades eyes)*
He said, "Throw out the nets	*(throwing motions)*
and you will catch fish."	*(nod yes)*
They caught so many fish	*(count on fingers)*
the net was very heavy	*(pretend to pull)*
Peter said to the others,	*(hands near mouth)*
"It is the Lord."	*(arms outstretched)*
The disciples pulled in the net	*(pretend to pull)*
and rowed to shore.	*(rowing motions)*
Jesus said to them,	*(hands near mouth)*
"Come and eat."	*(eating motions)*
Then the disciples knew for sure	*(nod head)*
that this was the risen Jesus.	*(point to palms)*

Children like echo pantomimes because they are actively involved in the story. Echo pantomimes help the children retain the lesson of the Bible story.

Alleluia Banner

Ask a parent or teacher who has a computer to print a 6′ long banner with the message "Jesus Is Risen. Alleluia." Computer programs are available to allow this to be done in large, block letters.

Assign each student to color all or part of one of the letters using markers. Encourage creativity. Some of the letters can be decorated with stripes or dots. A variety of colors can be used.

Ask the students to add Easter symbols such as a butterfly, caterpillar, sun, bird, or flower to the banner. The students can suggest other symbols as well.

Hang the alleluia banner in the school hallway or in another place where everyone can see it. Keep the banner displayed throughout the Easter season. The colorful artwork will help proclaim this great message in the days ahead.

Ascension Thursday

The cycle A gospel reading for Ascension Thursday (Matthew 28:16-20) reminds us that Jesus, although gone from sight, remains with us.

Discuss with the children some of the ways that Jesus is present in our lives; for example, through:

—people who help others in his name
—the gospel proclaimed at Mass
—Christians who tell others the good news
—the eucharist we share as a community
—the Holy Spirit who guides us
—the words and actions of his followers.

Have the children make a Bible verse chain to help them remember Ascension Thursday and Jesus' promise to be with us always. Provide eight colors of construction paper cut into 1" x 8 1/2" strips. Give each child one strip of each color. Have them print one word from the verse in Matthew 28:20—"And know that I am with you always"—on each strip.

The children assemble the Bible verse chains by making a circle with the first strip and securing it with tape or glue. Each strip is connected so that the chain spells out the Bible verse in the correct order.

This Bible verse chain encourages children to remember the feast of the Ascension and how Jesus remains with us today in many ways.

Class Prayer

In celebration of the Easter season, we praise God for the wondrous gift of life. The following prayer can help the children offer their thanks and praise to God.

Dear God,
A new day dawns
for us through the resurrection
of your Son, Jesus Christ.
He brings us new life.

We offer you this day
and each day of our lives.
Help us to see each new day
as a new beginning.

Help us to live today
as your Son showed us:
with faith in you,
with hope in your kingdom,
with love for you through love of others.

Send your Holy Spirit to guide us
and be with us in all that we do,
today and always.

Amen.

This type of prayer helps children keep in mind their call to live as followers of Jesus Christ, through the Holy Spirit, now and forever.

Church Poster

Pentecost is known as the birthday of the church. Filled with the Holy Spirit, the followers of Jesus proclaimed the good news to others. They lived in common, sharing with one another to meet the physical and spiritual needs of all. They truly formed "one body in Christ."

It is important for children to learn that the church today is a community of God's people. Through the church we are united not just to God, but to one another.

One visual way to help young children experience this idea of community is by having them work together to make a church poster. Use a large sheet of blue posterboard. At the top, place red self-stick letters to spell out "We Are Church." At the bottom, use the stickers to print "We Are Community."

Make copies of a pattern of both boy and girl figures, approximately 5" tall. The children contribute to the project by tracing and cutting out a figure from one of several different colors of construction paper. Have them add their names to the figures, using a fine black marker. Also, give each child a red heart sticker to add to their cut-out. Tell them that this symbolizes their love for God and others. Finally, allow each child to attach his or her figures to the posterboard. A glue stick works best.

Display this poster in the classroom. Make the connection between the cooperative effort that took place on this project with the sharing of time and talent that takes place in the church. Remind the children that they are church and are called to be church for one another.

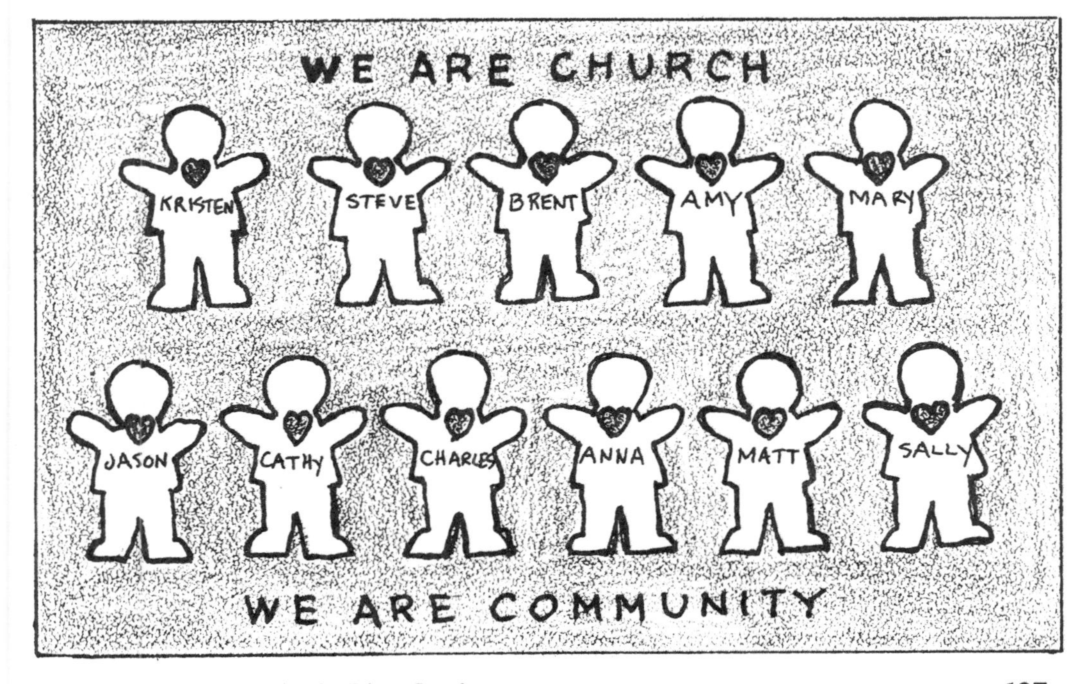

Fruits of the Spirit

Among the fruits of the Holy Spirit are love, joy, peace, patience, kindness, generosity, faithfulness, gentleness, and self-control. These fruits help us to live as Christians.

Read the passage from Galatians 5:22 which lists these fruits of the Spirit. Discuss with the students ways to apply these fruits to their own lives. Then encourage them to individualize the lesson even more by writing specific ways they can live one or more of the Spirit's fruits.

Provide copies of dove shape cutouts. Display the following sentence starters on the chalkboard. Ask the students to complete one sentence per dove. Encourage them to write as many sentences as time allows.

I show love when . . .

I show joy when . . .

I show peace when . . .

I show patience when . . .

I show kindness when . . .

I show generosity when . . .

I show faithfulness when . . .

I show gentleness when . . .

I show self-control when . . .

When completed, have the students glue their doves to a half-sheet of red construction paper. Display these pledges on the bulletin board as examples of how the students promise to live a life in the Spirit.

Decorated Dove

The dove is a traditional symbol of the Holy Spirit. When Jesus was baptized, the Holy Spirit is described as coming upon him like a dove. We, too, receive the Holy Spirit at baptism. A decorated dove can remind the children of this constant and everlasting gift.

Provide each child with a cutout of a white dove and a sheet of red construction paper for background. Have the children glue the dove in the middle of the paper. Below the dove, on the red construction paper, have them print "Gifted with the Spirit" in fine black marker.

To add decoration to the dove, give each child several 1 1/2" squares of white tissue paper. Demonstrate how to place the center of one tissue square around the end of a pencil and form it so the sides stand up. Tell the students to glue these formed tissue squares onto the dove. Covered with tissue, the dove takes on a three-dimensional look.

This craft project will help the students remember the presence of the Holy Spirit in their own lives.

Peace and Justice Litany

Inspired by the gift of the Spirit at Pentecost, we are called to bring about God's kingdom by working for peace and justice, both near and far. This peace and justice litany provides an opportunity for students to pray for the needs of other people. Choose six readers. The other students can participate by listening to the words and speaking the response.

Reader 1: Where children go to bed hungry at night . . .

All: **Lord, help us to bring hope.**

Reader 2: Where people are homeless . . .

All: **Lord, help us to bring hope.**

Reader 3: Where there are victims of discrimination and prejudice . . .

All: **Lord, help us to bring hope.**

Reader 4: Where disease and sickness take many lives . . .

All: **Lord, help us to bring hope.**

Reader 5: Where people live in poverty . . .

All: **Lord, help us to bring hope.**

Reader 6: Where wars tear apart families and pit nation against nation . . .

All: **Lord, help us to bring hope.**

This litany reminds the children that as Christians we must work for changes in our community, nation, and world so as to help those who live in poverty. We must see that all people have the basic needs so that they can live with dignity and hope.

Holy Spirit Prayer Service

Use the following prayer service as part of a lesson prior to Pentecost. It enables the students to pray together. An adult acts as the leader. Choose volunteers to do the readings. Encourage all the students to join together in the songs and the responses.

Opening Song

Holy Is the Spirit of the Lord (Young People's Glory and Praise).

Greeting

Leader: The feast of Pentecost is near. We come together to remember who we are as Christians and who we are called to be.

All: **We rejoice in the gift of the Spirit.**

Bible Reading

Reader 1: A reading from the First Letter to the Corinthians (12:4-7). There are different kinds of spiritual gifts but the same Spirit; there are different forms of service but the same Lord; there are different workings but the same God who produces all of them in everyone. To each individual the manifestation of the Spirit is given for some benefit. The word of the Lord.

All: **Thanks be to God.**

Petitions

Reader 2: May we witness the teachings of Jesus Christ by the way we live our lives.

All: **Holy Spirit, guide us.**

Reader 3: May we gather together as a community of faith to worship and give God praise.

All: **Holy Spirit, guide us.**

Reader 4: May we support and affirm one another as we seek God's will in our lives.

All: **Holy Spirit, guide us.**

Reader 5: May each of us use our gifts for the good of all people.

All: **Holy Spirit, guide us.**

Reader 6: May we work together for peace and justice in the world.

All: **Holy Spirit, guide us.**

Closing Prayer and Blessing

Leader: Holy Spirit, hear our prayers. Help us to live as one body in Christ. Open our minds and hearts to the needs of others. We ask this in your name.

All: **Amen.**

Closing Song:

Spirit of God, Come to Us (Young People's Glory and Praise II).

Chapter 5

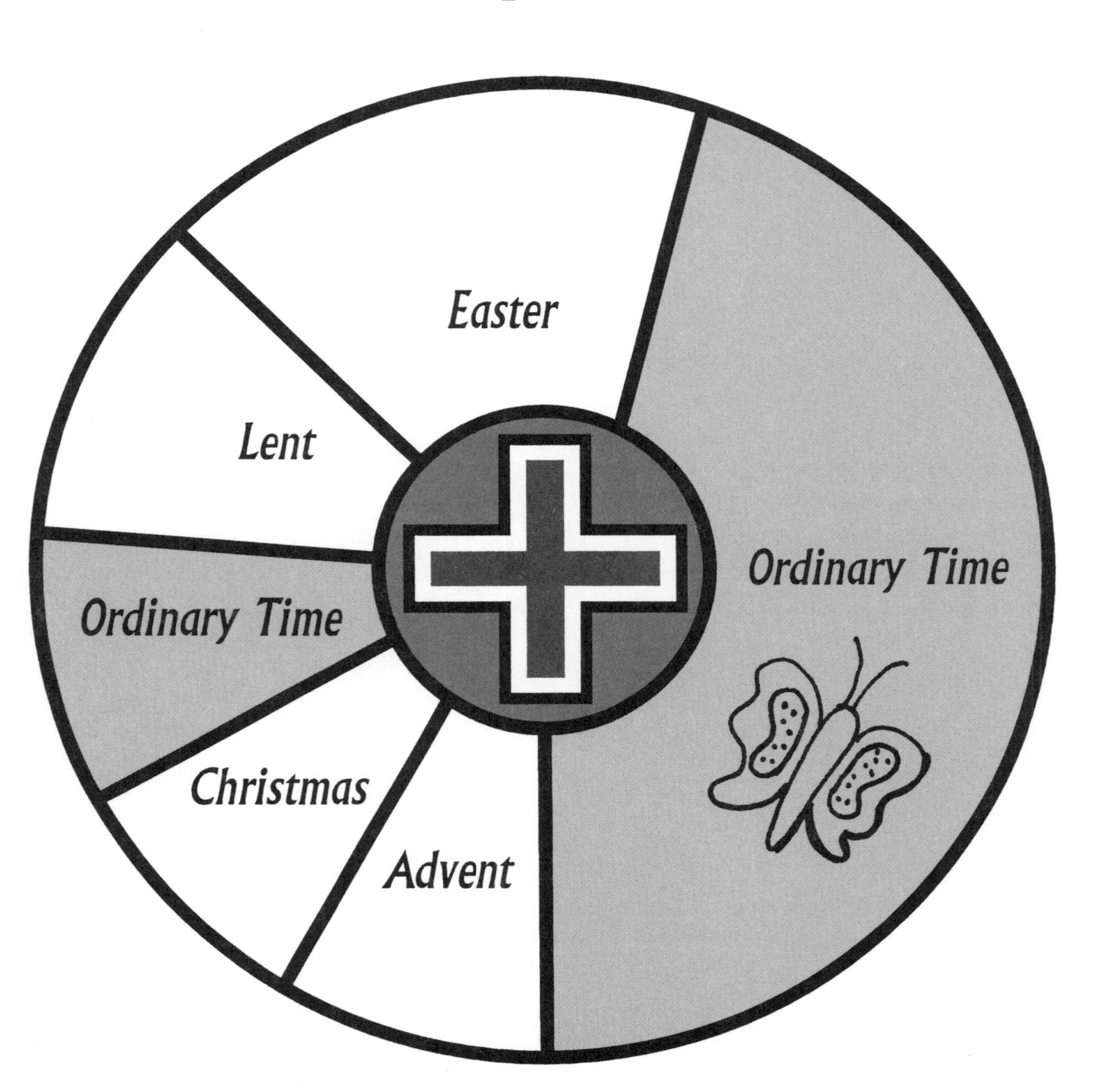

~Ordinary Time~

We Share the Good News

Go into the whole world
and proclaim the gospel.
~Mark 16:15~

Ordinary refers to the word ordinal, which means "counted time". The season of Ordinary Time reflects the beauty and goodness of our everyday lives: our work, our relationships, our fears, our joys. During Ordinary Time, no particular theme is covered. Rather, we hear an overall sense of Jesus' ministry in the scripture readings. We are clearly challenged with Jesus' call to discipleship.

There are actually two parts to the season of Ordinary Time. The first and shorter part occurs from the end of the Christmas season until the beginning of Lent. The longer part is from Pentecost until the beginning of Advent.

The scripture readings of Ordinary Time—as with the rest of the Church Year—are on a three-year cycle. In cycle A the stories from Matthew's gospel are featured. In cycle B the focus is on the gospel of Mark. During cycle C we listen to the gospel of Luke. John's gospel is read during the Lent and Easter seasons of all three years. Dividing the Sunday gospel readings into a three-year cycle allows the church to receive broad flavor of these New Testament readings.

The season of Ordinary Time is also marked by the feast days of many people the world once knew as ordinary, but we now call extraordinary—the saints. We use this time to examine how these people lived the message of Jesus Christ. We try to imitate their examples.

Nourished by the word of God, we go forth to live as God's people. The gospel message is to be lived in our ordinary lives as Christians.

Apostles' Meditation

How would you feel if Jesus approached you and asked you to follow? Jesus' call of his apostles is our call as well.

Read to the students the following paraphrase of Mark 1:16-20. Ask the students to close their eyes and imagine that they are there the day Jesus walked along the seashore and called his first followers.

If possible, play a recording of background sound effects of waves coming ashore. Reflective instrumental music is also enhancing. Read the story in a deliberate style. Pause often to allow the students to absorb the scene and the power of Jesus' words.

> It was mid-afternoon as the man walked along the shore of the sea of Galilee. His eyes absorbed the bright sunlight as it struck the water. He heard the sound of seagulls as they circled overhead. This man from Nazareth looked out over the water as far as he could see. This man was Jesus.
>
> Soon he saw boats appear on the horizon. The fishermen were returning from a day at sea. The boats grew larger and larger in appearance as they came closer to shore. People came from everywhere along the docks to unload the fish from each boat. Out of the way, Jesus waited, watched, until the last of the fish was carried away.
>
> Then he walked up to the first boat. In the hull stood a man, his face weathered by the sun and wind. Behind him stood another man with similar features. They were brothers. Jesus called, "Simon Peter and Andrew. Come, follow me."
>
> "We are coming, Lord," they replied. Peter and Andrew dropped their nets and walked to where Jesus waited.
>
> They followed Jesus further along the seashore. He stopped at another fishing boat. Two other brothers, James and John, were mending their nets. He called to them, "James and John, follow me." They left their father Zebedee and their hired workers in the boat and followed him.
>
> Today, Jesus calls you. What do you need to leave behind? "Come," Jesus calls to you. "Come, follow me." How will you answer him?

Provide some additional time for quiet refection. Do not follow this meditation with discussion. Rather allow the students to come to a personal resolution to Jesus' invitation.

Peace and Justice Pledge

On All Saints Day we hear the Beatitudes proclaimed in the gospel reading. All followers of Jesus Christ are to live these beatitude values. We must work to become beatitude people.

Read Matthew 5:3-12 to the students. Lead a discussion about what it means to bring peace to the world and to work for the rights of others. Encourage the students to suggest practical ways they can do this in their own lives. Tell them they can enact one or more of the ideas mentioned by their classmates.

This lesson on peace and justice can be personalized for the students by filling out a pledge card like the one below. Print these pledge statements on a half-sheet of paper and make one copy for each student.

Peace and Justice Pledge

I,______________________________, promise to work for peace and justice at home and in my community. I pledge that I will stand up for justice especially when______________________________

____.

One thing I promise to do to help settle disagreements peacefully is

____.

I promise to do this because I am a Christian who wants to live as Jesus did.

____

Signature

Taking this type of pledge reminds the students to be aware of and practice their responsibilities as Christians. It takes learning beyond the classroom into their everyday lives.

Jesus' Song

The miracle stories shared in the gospels tell how Jesus cured the lame, gave sight to the blind, and raised the dead. The kingdom of God is present in the actions of Jesus Christ.

Jesus' cure of the paralytic in Mark 2:1-12 revealed an additional truth about Jesus: he had power to not only to cure people, but to forgive their sins as well. He was indeed the Son of God.

Help young children learn the lesson of this story and of Jesus' other healings. Sing the following lyrics to the tune of "Mary had a Little Lamb."

Jesus came to teach us all,
teach us all, teach us all.
Jesus came to teach us all.
He is the Son of God.

Jesus came to heal the sick,
heal the sick, heal the sick.
Jesus came to heal the sick.
He is the Son of God.

Jesus came to show God's love,
show God's love, show God's love.
Jesus came to show God's love.
He is the Son of God.

This is a catchy song that the children quickly learn. Singing helps children understand how a story from long ago impacts their lives today.

Trinity Sunday

Belief in the Trinity is at the heart of our faith. Lead a discussion about the three persons in one God—Father, Son, and Holy Spirit—in conjunction with the celebration of Trinity Sunday.

The best type of discussion involves asking students questions at their level of understanding. This engages their interest and attention. Sample points for discussion include:

- Explain that there are three persons in one God. (Call on the children to name them.)

- Remind the children that God the Father is also known as Creator. (Call on the children to list some of the things that God has made.)

- Tell the children that God's greatest gift is the gift of Jesus Christ, God the Son. (Call on the children to recall some of the things that Jesus taught us.)

- Point out that the Holy Spirit lives in our church and in our hearts. (Call on the children to share some of the ways the Holy Spirit helps; for example, in making good choices and in praying.)

- Explain that the sign of the cross helps us to show our belief in the Trinity. (Call on the children to share times they make the sign of the cross.)

Expand on these points. Ask the children to develop their own related questions. Use these and additional questions to help further a lesson on the Blessed Trinity.

Children's Prayer

Our lives and the life of the church is modeled in the community of faith that is the Trinity—Father, Son, and Holy Spirit. We offer prayers in the name of the Blessed Trinity at each liturgy. The following prayer can be used with the children on or near Trinity Sunday to celebrate, praise, worship, and thank our Triune God.

God, the Father,
We honor you as the Father of us all
and thank you for your great love for us.
May we remember that each of us
is created in your image and likeness.
We praise you for the gift of your creation
and glorify your name above all things.

God, the Son,
We thank you for giving your life
that we might have new life through you.
Help us to walk in your way
even as it means taking up our own crosses.
May we proclaim the good news of your life,
death, and resurrection to all we encounter.

God, the Holy Spirit,
We know that you live in our hearts
and in our church community.
Be with us and guide us
in all things.
Enable us to be people of hope
and people of peace.

Amen.

Praise Psalm

The season of Ordinary Time is a great occasion to praise God for the "ordinary" gifts we often take for granted: love, music, nature, joy, mercy, forgiveness, and faith. Ordinary indeed!

Pray this psalm of praise—based on Psalm 145—together with the children. Divide the class into a left side and a right side and have the children pray this prayer in turn.

Left: I will extol you, O my God and King,
and I will bless your name forever and ever.

Right: Every day will I bless you,
and I will praise your name forever and ever.

Left: Great is the LORD and highly to be praised.
His greatness is unsearchable.

Right: Generation after generation praises your works
and proclaims your might.

Left: The LORD is gracious and merciful,
slow to anger and of great kindness.

Right: The LORD is good to all and compassionate toward all his works.

Left: Let all your works give you thanks, O LORD,
and let your faithful ones bless you.

Right: Your kingdom is a kingdom for all ages,
and your dominion endures through all generations.

This method of praying a psalm helps the children give glory and praise to God.

Helping Hands

Read or paraphrase the story of the Good Samaritan (Luke 10:29-42). Then lead a class discussion delving into the meaning of the story: Who is it that needs our help? How can we help these people in need? Encourage the children to contribute ideas such as making a new child feel welcome, doing chores for a neighbor, and praying for others.

After the discussion have the students make a helping hands craft to remind them to live out the example of this story. Give each student a half-sheet of light-colored construction paper and a thin black marker. Tell them to spread their fingers wide apart and trace the shapes of both left and right hands on the paper. (If the students work in pairs, one person can hold the paper while the other traces.) Have them write their first name on the tracing of their left hand and their last name on the tracing of their right hand and cut them out.

Next, distribute full-sheets of bright-colored construction paper. Have them print the words "I can help others" at the bottom of this paper and then glue their hand cutouts above the words. Be prepared to help the children with one or more of these steps.

This activity encourages the children to think of ways they can help, like the good Samaritan. Displaying the craft project at home will help them remember to keep their promises.

Summer Samaritans

The gospel of Luke is sometimes known as the "gospel of mercy." In Luke 10, Jesus challenges us to expand our concept of neighbor to include even those people we do not know. Summer Samaritans is a service project that helps children to live this important message.

Summer months can be brutally hot. For some people, including those with health problems and the elderly, this heat can be life-threatening. The inside temperature can reach over 100 degrees, leading to heat stroke or other serious health problems. In the Summer Samaritans project, the children collect monetary donations to provide electric fans for those who need them.

Check with local agencies to see if such a project is in place in the community. If so, these agencies know where the needs exist and will purchase and deliver the fans. Sometimes police departments are involved in this outreach project.

Set a goal for your group; for example, to collect enough money to buy one fan from each class. Discuss with the children sources for earning money. Encourage the children to contribute money to this project from allowances, garage sales, neighborhood chores, or birthday gifts. Keep a container in the classroom to collect all donations.

This project is an example of seeking out the needs of others and striving to meet those needs in the name of Jesus.

Living the Our Father

We pray the Lord's Prayer each time we gather for eucharist. Help the children understand the meaning of the Our Father and to live what we pray. Share these ideas for enacting each part of the Our Father. Encourage the students to contribute more of their own ideas.

Our Father, who is in heaven,
—remember that we are all God's children
—say hello to someone who is new or lonely
—stand up for another child who is being teased

Hallowed be your name.
—remember to pray each day
—thank God for sending us Jesus
—praise God for all creation

Your kingdom come; your will be done on earth
as it is in heaven.
—put God first
—tell someone about Jesus
—be kind to another person

Give us this day our daily bread;
—do our best each day
—say grace before meals
—help those who are hungry

And forgive us our trespasses as we forgive those
who trespass against us.
—ask God's forgiveness
—say the Act of Sorrow
—forgive someone who has been mean

And lead us not into temptation, but deliver us from evil.
—turn away from selfishness
—pray that God will always be with us
—try to act as Jesus taught

Students learn from their peers. Write some of the shared ideas on the board. You may wish to have them jot down some of these ideas in their notebooks. Periodically check with the students to see how well they are following their plans.

Bible Puzzles

Use this Bible puzzle activity to help the students become more familiar with the gospel of John.

Cut out shapes of items from colored posterboard related to a particular gospel verse (see examples, below). Write the Bible verse and citation on the appropriate shape. Then cut each shape into two puzzle-like pieces. Give one puzzle piece to each child. Tell them to mingle around the room until they find the other child with the interlocking piece that spells out the complete Bible verse.

After all the verses are matched up, ask the children to meet in the large group with their partner and share with everyone else their Bible verse and item.

Suitable items and corresponding Bible verses for puzzle pieces include:

BREAD	I am the bread of life. (6:35)
HEART	Love one another. (15:17)
SHEEP	I am the Good Shepherd. (10:11)
FISH	Follow me. (1:43)
BUTTERFLY	I am the resurrection and the life. (11:25)
CROSS	God gave his only Son. (3:16)
SUN	I am the light of the world. (8:12)

This activity can be repeated several times. Just mix up the pieces each round. Save the discussion until the very end. This is a fun way for children to learn Bible verses from John's gospel.

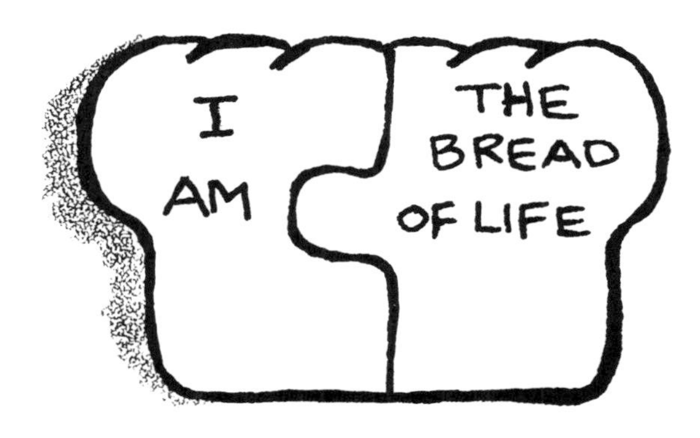

Mary Holy Card

The Assumption of Mary is celebrated on August 15 during the season of Ordinary Time. On this feast day we remember that Mary was taken into heaven body and soul. We can pray to Mary and ask her for her prayers on our behalf.

Distribute Mary holy cards to the children on or near the feast of the Assumption to remind them that Mary is the mother of God and our mother, too. One inexpensive and simple way to make Mary holy cards is by using old Christmas cards that feature nativity scenes of Mary with the baby Jesus.

Cut out 2 1/2" x 4" pieces of posterboard. Then, cut out pictures of Mary from the Christmas cards. Center and glue the pictures on the posterboard. Print "August 15—Feast of the Assumption" on the back of the card. The variety of Mary images means that many different holy cards will be available for the children to look at and share.

Distribute the holy cards after a lesson on the Assumption. Holy cards are a great way to celebrate the holy day and a good reminder for the children to attend Mass on that day.

Lost Sheep Pantomime

The parable of the lost sheep (Luke 15:1-7) helps children to learn about God's never-ending love. It can be shared with children using an echo pantomime format. The children echo the words and actions of the teacher for each line.

One day Jesus was teaching	*(hands cup mouth)*
those who followed him.	*(walk in place)*
If a shepherd has 100 sheep	*(count on fingers)*
and one gets lost,	*(hold up one finger)*
the shepherd will leave 99	*(walk in place)*
and search for the stray.	*(shade eyes with hand)*
When he finds the sheep	*(arms outstretched)*
he rejoices over it.	*(clap hands)*
It is the same way	*(nod head)*
with our heavenly Father.	*(point upward)*
God does not want	*(shake head no)*
even one of us to be lost.	*(hold up one finger)*
God loves everyone.	*(hug self)*

An echo pantomime is an exciting way of working with children and Bible stories. It allows children to participate in the telling of the story.

Following St. Francis

The feast of St. Francis is celebrated on October 4. The prayer of St. Francis is a beautiful prayer that can help students understand how we are called to live as Christians. The following activity helps upper elementary students learn how to put the words of this prayer into action.

Print the six phrases of the prayer that begin with the word "where" on individual slips of paper. Divide the students into groups of three or four and have one person from each group randomly select one slip of paper.

Ask the groups to discuss the meaning of their phrase and to think of situations involving kids their own age in which they could enact what the phrase says. Here are some ideas that can be shared with the students as needed:

Where there is hatred, let me bring love.

You hear a group of girls and boys talking about a member of your class. You hear them say: "I just can't stand him. He is so fat, has such funny clothes, is so stupid." What can you say to help these individuals stop hating and begin loving? What could you do to bring love to the boy or girl they dislike?

Where there is injury, let me bring pardon.

Someone in your class you thought of as a friend gives a party, but you are not invited. What do you do the next time you see that person?

Where there is doubt, let me bring faith.

A friend of yours says she is not really sure there is a God. Her prayers never seem to be answered. And there is so much trouble in the world. How can we know God is really there? What can you say to that person?

Where there is despair, let me bring hope.

A friend of yours is discouraged. He is upset because everything seems to be going wrong. His grades in school are down. His parents are after him to work harder. He is doing the best he can and doesn't know how to improve. Whatever he tries seems to turn out wrong. He wonders if God cares about him. What do you say to your friend?

Where there is darkness, let me bring light.

You have a friend whose parents are going through a divorce. Her whole life is upset and she cannot imagine things will ever be peaceful and joyful again. How can you help?

Where there is sadness, let me bring joy.

Your brother has been practicing very hard to make a particular team. When he comes home on the day of the tryouts he goes running up to his room and shuts the door. You know he did not make the team. What can you do?

Allow the groups sufficient time for discussion. Then ask each group to share their phrase, situation, and course of action. This extends the benefit of the small group discussions to the entire class.

Coat Collection

Warm coats are a necessity for children in the cold of winter. However, it is often impossible for many for families to afford new winter coats. Concurrently many other children outgrow coats that are still warm and serviceable. A school or parish collection can help provide winter coats for children who need them. Consider beginning this service project on October 4, the feast day of St. Francis.

Ask families to donate outgrown children's coats that are in good condition. Set a collection date and place and arrange to staff it with volunteers. Sometimes a dry cleaning business will offer to clean the coats at no cost. Each coat should also be clearly marked with size.

The best way to handle the distribution of the coats is to give them to a church or charitable organization that is not in your immediate area. By doing this, a child is less likely to have his or her "new" winter jacket recognized by the child who donated it. Encourage children and adults alike to participate in the project. This is practical service in the spirit of St. Francis that directly benefits everyone.

Heart Collage

It is important for children to know God's love for them. They need to know that each of them is a special and wonderful creation of God. Only when they feel secure in God's unconditional love will they be able to reach out to love God and love others. The gospel story of Jesus' blessing the children (Mark 10:13-16) helps to that end. Look up the story in the Bible and read it to the class.

A way to help children remember this story is with a heart collage. Distribute a sheet of 8 1/2" x 11" red construction paper to each child and have them trace and cut out a large heart. A black line with crayon or marker can be drawn around the edge of the heart for a decorative effect.

Next, give each child a half-sheet of white, unlined paper and have them trace and cut out a smaller heart. On the smaller heart ask them to print the words "Jesus loves the children" and glue it to the center of the larger heart.

Finally, provide an assortment of magazines. Have the children select photos of children, cut them out, and glue them onto the larger heart as well. Photos can be precut for younger children.

This craft is a reminder to the children that Jesus truly loves them. The words and pictures express this message.

Thank You Photos

The story of the one leper who came back to say thank you to Jesus (Luke 17:11-19) reminds us that we too must thank God for the many gifts we have received.

To help the children learn how to express thankfulness to God, cut out photos from magazines, travel brochures, and garden catalogs of some of these gifts; for example:

people	fruit
families	trees
children	lakes
animals	sunsets
birds	mountains
flowers	

Glue each photo to a slightly larger piece of posterboard to form a frame. Next, carefully cover the photos with clear self-adhesive paper to protect them from wear and tear and guarantee longer use.

In class, lead a discussion on God's gifts. Brainstorm with them a list of the many gifts of creation.

After the discussion, ask each child to select one of the photos. (You or the adult leader should do so also.) Then begin a thank you prayer. Read the story of the ten lepers. Ask each child to say thank you to God for the gift on their photo.

All Saints Day Litany

All Saints Day is celebrated on November 1. This is the day that the church recognizes the countless number of people who lived good and holy lives on earth and are now living in the peace of heaven. These are the saints with a small "s" who have not been singled out with their own feast day on the church calendar.

To mark this occasion, have the children write their own litany of the saints using both canonized saints who are familiar to them as well as mentioning "all holy men and women". Ask the children to suggest names of favorite saints. Write these names on the chalkboard. Have the students add a descriptive phrase about each saint.

Use the following litany as a classroom prayer or develop your own based on the students' suggestions. Choose volunteers to read the name and description of each saint. The rest of the children offer the response.

Reader 1: St. Martin de Porres,
servant of the poor,
All: **pray for us.**

Reader 2: St. Thérèse,
person of simplicity,
All: **pray for us.**

Reader 3: St. Andrew,
apostle of Jesus,
All: **pray for us.**

Reader 4: St. Rose Duchesne,
friend of native Americans,
All: **pray for us.**

Reader 5: St. Dominic,
preacher of God's word,
All: **pray for us.**

Reader 6:	St. Elizabeth of Portugal, seeker of peace,
All:	**pray for us.**
Reader 7:	St. Isidore, patron of farmers,
All:	**pray for us.**
Reader 8:	St. Catherine of Siena, doctor of the church,
All:	**pray for us.**
Reader 9:	St. John Bosco, educator of youth,
All:	**pray for us.**
Reader 10:	All holy men and women, models of faith,
All:	**pray for us.**

This litany helps us to appreciate the examples of Christians who have lived before us: both those whose stories are familiar to us and those whose stories we may have never heard.

Commandment Prayer Service

This prayer service highlights the greatest commandment as reiterated by Jesus: love of God and love of neighbor. One way to conduct this service is for you or another adult to act as the leader. Select volunteers to read the bible reading and the intercessions. All the students offer the responses.

Opening Song

This Is The Day (Young People's Glory and Praise)

Greeting

Leader: The Lord be with you.

All: **And also with you.**

Opening Prayer

Leader: Let us pray. Almighty God, we gather together today to give glory and praise to your name. Thank you for sending us your Son, Jesus Christ. Help us to follow him in all things with the help of your guiding Spirit. We ask this in your name.

All: **Amen.**

Bible Reading

Reader 1: A reading from the gospel of Matthew (22:37-39): Jesus said to him, "You shall love the Lord, your God, with all your heart, with all your soul, and with all your mind. This is the greatest and the first commandment. The second is like it: You shall love your neighbor as yourself." The word of the Lord.

All: **Thanks be to God.**

Intercessions

Leader: We pray that the love of Jesus Christ may increase in our lives.

Reader 2: Jesus, you came not to be served, but to serve others; help us to serve others in your name.

All: **Lord, hear our prayer.**

Reader 3: Jesus you loved others, especially the poor and outcast; help us to love and care for all people.

All: **Lord, hear our prayer.**

Reader 4: Jesus, you healed those who were sick; help us to minister to those who are ill in mind and body.

All: **Lord, hear our prayer.**

Reader 5: Jesus, you came to tell us about the Father's love; help us to tell others.

All: **Lord, hear our prayer.**

Reader 6: Jesus, you prayed to the Father; help us to take time to pray each day.

All: **Lord, hear our prayer.**

Lord's Prayer

Leader: Let us pray together the prayer that the Lord taught us.

All: **Our Father . . .**

Concluding Prayer

Leader: Loving Father, we ask your help to follow the command that you gave us. May others come to know your love through all we say and do. We make this prayer in the name of your Son.

All: **Amen.**

Concluding Song

This Is My Commandment (Young People's Glory and Praise)

Walk in Love

The commandments are guides to help us to grow in God's love. A poster display is a terrific idea to help children remember that Christians are called to love others. Cut large block letters from blue construction paper to spell "Walk in Love." Glue the letters to a sheet of white poster board.

Provide each child with a footprint pattern cut from a variety of brightly colored of construction paper. Have the children print their names on the footprints as a sign that they will follow Jesus' way of love. Glue the footprints to the poster. This makes a bright and colorful class display that is personalized because the children's names are included. It reminds us to walk in love with Jesus.

Zacchaeus' Rhyme

The story of Zacchaeus from Luke 19:1-10 is a story of conversion and change of heart. It is read from cycle C on the thirty-first Sunday of the Church Year. Look up the story in the Bible and read or paraphrase it for the children.

Young children can be further introduced to this gospel story through an action rhyme. Have the children follow the leader's promptings and do the accompanying motions to fit the words of the rhyme as they are read aloud.

Zacchaeus was short so he climbed a tree.	*(climbing motions)*
Jesus said, "Come on down and be with me."	*(beckon with arm)*
Zacchaeus told him, "No more will I cheat	*(shake head no)*
And to help the poor will I seek."	*(arms outstretched)*
Zacchaeus changed his heart that day;	*(hands over heart)*
When Jesus came to his house to stay.	*(point to palms)*

Children love to be involved and learn in this way. The actions help this gospel reading to come alive for children.

St. Rose Duchesne

St. Rose Duchesne is a recently canonized American saint. Spend some class time on or near her feast day, November 18, sharing some of her life story with the students. Here is a brief summary you can read or paraphrase:

> St. Rose came to the United States from France. She lived in Missouri and ministered to people there, but had a deep longing to work directly with the Native American population. In 1841, at age 71, she was finally able to fulfill that dream by going to Kansas to teach the Potawatomi tribe.
>
> She told the Potawatomi people about God's love and about Jesus Christ, and she founded a school for the children. But her age and health soon overcame her and she was called back to her motherhouse where she spent the last years of her life. "God knows the reason for this recall," she said, "and that is enough."
>
> St. Rose died on November 18, 1852.

Encourage the students to learn about St. Rose Duchesne and complete one of the following projects:

—study the everyday nineteenth century life of the Potawatomi tribe

—draw a picture of St. Rose teaching the children

—make a model of a typical Native American village

—watch a video about St. Rose

—discuss how God calls each of us to follow him

—explore the idea that with God all things are possible

Also, call on St. Rose Duchesne as an intercessor throughout the month of November.

Sharing Gifts

Each of us is called to use the gifts that have been given to us by God. This is the sum of the lesson of the parable of the talents (Matthew 25:14-30): stewardship is to be a way of life.

Read or paraphrase this parable for the children. Help them understand the meaning of stewardship in relationship to their personal gifts. Discuss with them the three-fold meaning of stewardship: the giving of time, talent, and treasure. Listed below are some discussion starters:

Time

It is important to help students understand that we are to reserve time for what is really important. Ask:

- What are some ways we spend our time? (i.e., eating, sleeping, school, television, playing, chores)

- What are some other important activities we must reserve time for? (i.e., going to Mass, praying, helping others)

- How can we make more time for these important things? (i.e., watching less television, participating in fewer activities)

Talent

Help the students recognize their own individual talents and how they can share them with others. Ask:

- What are some abilities God has given you? (i.e., art, academics, sports)

- How can you share these abilities with others? (i.e., draw a picture for a grandparent, help a younger child with homework, help coach a team)

Treasure

Point out the responsibility that all Christians have to share our financial and material resources in support of the local parish and all people in need. Ask:

- What are some expenses of our parish? (i.e., living expenses for priests, heating and air conditioning, building maintenance, school subsidy)

• Where does the money come from for these and other parish expenses? (mainly from parishioners through the regular Sunday collection)

• What are some other worthy causes that need our monetary support? (i.e., Holy Childhood Association, Catholic Relief Services, food pantries)

• What are ways for children to earn money? (i.e., allowances, birthday gifts, bake sale, chores)

A discussion of this kind will help the students understand the concept of stewardship and how it is to be personalized through their own words and actions.

Christ the King Prayer

The feast of Christ the King is celebrated during Ordinary Time on the last Sunday of the Church Year. It is a reminder that Jesus Christ is Ruler above all rulers, King above all kings. We are to honor and praise him alone. The following action prayer helps young children to celebrate this feast. Demonstrate the response actions before beginning (lift arms, palms open). Invite all the children to respond and do the actions.

Leader:	Christ is king of our hearts.	*(point to heart)*
	Christ is the king of our homes.	*(make roof out of arms and hands)*
All:	**We thank you, Jesus our king.**	*(lift arms, palms open)*
Leader:	For our family and friends,	
All:	**We thank you, Jesus our king.**	*(lift arms, palms open)*
Leader:	For our beautiful world,	
All:	**We thank you, Jesus our king.**	*(lift arms, palms open)*
Leader:	For the clothes we wear and the clothes we share,	
All:	**We thank you, Jesus our king.**	*(lift arms, palms open)*
Leader:	For pets and toys and friends to play with,	
All:	**We thank you, Jesus our king.**	*(lift arms, palms open)*
Leader:	For love and laughter,	
All:	**We thank you, Jesus our king.**	*(lift arms, palms open)*
Leader:	Christ is the king of our hearts.	*(point to heart)*
	Christ is king of our homes.	*(make a roof out of arms and hands)*
All:	**We thank you, Jesus our king.**	*(lift arms, palms open)*

This prayer with actions reminds us that Jesus Christ is the source of all good things in our lives.

Service to Others

The gospel reading for cycle A on the feast of Christ the King (Matthew 25:31-46) reminds us that we are to help the poor with their physical and spiritual needs.

Many millions of Americans live in poverty. The Campaign for Human Development is an organization sponsored by the United States Catholic Conference. The U.S. bishops created this campaign to provide grants and loans to poor communities in order to help break the cycle of poverty.

Explain something about the efforts of the Campaign for Human Development. Encourage the students to think of ways to earn money and donate it to this collection. Connect this service project with a lesson on Christ the King. Ideas for earning money include:

- sponsoring a walk-a-thon
- doing extra chores
- staging a class bake sale
- selling candy
- collecting donations
- recycling
- holding a school carnival for younger children

This is a project where children learn by doing. Assure the children that the money collected for the Campaign for Human Development will be used in a variety of ways to help those people with special needs.

Permissions and Acknowledgments

Chapter 1

"Living Advent Wreath" is excerpted from Eunice M. Mello, "A Living Advent Wreath for Teens", *Catechist*, November/December 1991, pp. 35-6. Used with permission of the publisher: Peter Li Education Group, 330 Progress Rd., Dayton, OH 45449.

Chapter 2

"Christmas Beatitudes" is excerpted from Estelle Lane, "The Joy of Hope" in *Creative Ideas for Advent, Volume 2*, ed. by Robert and Linda Davison (Prescott, AZ: Educational Ministries, Inc., 1986), p. 73.

Chapter 3

"Cross Strip Calendar" is excerpted from Sharon Lee, *Hosanna!* (Los Angeles, CA: Franciscan Communications, 1988), p. 10.

"Choral Reading" is excerpted from Jeanette Dall, "Hosanna to the King," *Shining Star*, February/March/April, 1992. Used with permission of Shining Star, P.O. Box 299, Carthage, IL 62321.

"Agape Service" is excerpted from . . . *And These Thy Gifts—Gift of Life Teacher Guide* (Huntington, IN: Our Sunday Visitor, Inc., 1982) p. 214.

"Remembering with Rocks" is excerpted from Kathie Frost, "Remembering with Rocks," *Religion Teacher's Journal*, March 1993, p. 35.

"Good Friday Story" is reprinted by permission from *Group Magazine*, © copyright 1992, Group Publishing, Box 481, Loveland, CO 80539.

Chapter 4

"Intention Tree" is adapted from Barbara J. Decker, "Intention Tree Idea Sheet" (New Orleans, LA: Resurrection of Our Lord School, 1993; St. Dominic School, 1994).

"Symbol Prayer" is from Mary Jo Tully and Sr. Mary Fearon, R.S.M, *Focus on Belonging Program Manual, Grade 2* (Dubuque, IA: Brown-ROA, 1981), p. 185. Reprinted with limited permission.

"Fruit of the Spirit" is excerpted from Maria Romero, O.P., M.Div. and Corinne Sanders, O.P., M.S., *Loving* (Kansas City, MO: Sheed and Ward, 1989), p. 29.

"Decorated Dove" is excerpted from Dyan Beller, *Creative Bible Crafts* (San Diego, CA: Rainbow Books, 1991), p. 24.

Chapter 5

"Peace and Justice Pledge" is excerpted from Anne Marie Mongoven, O.P., Ph.D. and Maureen Gallagher, Ph.D, *Living Waters Manual, Grade 4* (Allen, TX: Tabor Publishing, 1992), p. 136.

"Following St. Francis" is excerpted from Mary Lou Kownacki, O.S.B. with Carol Clark, *Let Peace Begin with Me* (Mystic, CT: Twenty-Third Publications, 1989), pp. 12-13.

"Walk in Love" is excerpted from Carole MacKenthun, R.S.M. and Paulinus Dwyer, O.P., *Love* (Carthage, IL: Shining Star Publications, 1986), p.40. Used by permission of Shining Star, P.O. Box 299, Carthage, IL 62321.

"Christ the King Prayer" is excerpted from *Promise* (Dayton, OH: Pflaum Student Magazines, 1987), p. 1.